# Spokesongs

## Bicycle Adventures on Three Continents

### Willie Weir

pineleaf productions
Seattle, Washington

**Spokesongs:** Bicycle Adventures on Three Continents

Copyright © 1997 Willie Weir

Printed in the United States of America

First printing April, 1997

Library of Congress Catalog Card Number 97-065213

ISBN: 0-9656792-6-8

Cover photos:  Author climbing Rama's Gate—South Africa
School girls—Himachal Pradesh, India
Street scene—Ljubljana, Slovenia

Cover design, book design, map illustrations by Kat Marriner

The material in this book was originally aired on public radio station KUOW in Seattle, Washington.

The India section was originally published as *Cycling India: Letters From the Road.*

Published by:

Pineleaf Productions
7812 Stone Avenue N
Seattle, WA 98103
PineleafPr@aol.com

*A portion of the profits from the sale of this book are donated to NowBike, a non-profit bicycle advocacy organization in Washington state.*

To my brother, Jeff,

for whom I began to write

# Table of contents

# South Africa

# The Balkans

# Preface

I can't remember precisely when my love affair with bicycle travel began: Perhaps it was while riding my three-speed Schwinn down to Thrifty drugstore to purchase fifteen-cent, triple-scoop ice cream cones that melted down my arm before I got half-way across the parking lot; or while riding my yellow, ten-speed Vista Esquire to the bowling alley with my fourteen-pound, name-engraved bowling ball perched on the top tube; or perhaps years later as a courier in Seattle, Washington, dodging city traffic, little old ladies and attorneys on my Raleigh mountain bike. But when push comes to shove, I'd have to pin it down to a journey across the United States with my childhood buddy, Thomas. We didn't really know what we were doing—little planning, less money, and no training. We simply pedaled off from Seaside, Oregon in July on our Univega Gran Turismo touring bikes and two months later found ourselves cycling down 2nd Avenue in New York City.

That trip was sixteen years, twenty-two countries and some 35,000 miles ago.

I have always kept my journals in the form of letters home to my brother, Jeff—my devoted audience of one. In 1994 my audience dramatically expanded with the opportunity to write commentaries for public radio station, KUOW in Seattle, Washington. This book contains the commentaries I wrote from three separate journeys: India in 1994, South Africa in 1995, and the Balkans in 1996. They by no means begin to encompass the enormity and diversity of the experiences I had; that would take several volumes. I hope you enjoy them for what they are—fifty-nine verbal songs of the road. If these "spokesongs" make you smile or laugh or wonder, or inspire you to explore the world outside the organized tour packages and resorts of the world—my time has been well spent.

# India

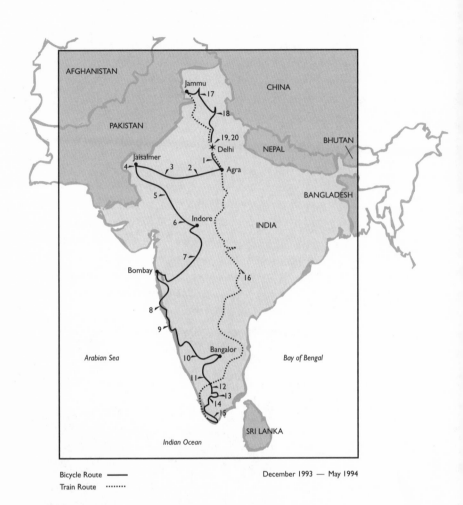

Bicycle Route ——
Train Route ⋯⋯⋯

December 1993 — May 1994

## Map Key

1 ⏤ Road Warrior
2 ⏤ Bicycle Circus
3 ⏤ Charlie Brown Plays Cricket
4 ⏤ Camels
5 ⏤ A Night in Jail
6 ⏤ The Bhagvati Binge
7 ⏤ I Am God
8 ⏤ Back Roads and Back Waters
9 ⏤ Beached in Goa
10 ⏤ Ear Cleaners

11 ⏤ Climb Every Mountain
12 ⏤ The Five Questions
13 ⏤ Arnold
14 ⏤ The Magic Word
15 ⏤ Bent into Shape
16 ⏤ The Himsagar Express
17 ⏤ A Shepherd's Life For Me
18 ⏤ Jalori Pass
19 ⏤ Conned
20 ⏤ Back to Delhi

In 1993, on the last day of a four-month bicycle tour in New Zealand, I met another cyclist, a Frenchman, and we swapped travel stories. He had recently traveled with his girlfriend through India. He couldn't stop talking about this strange, maddening, wonderful country. "You have to go there," he insisted. "I will," I said, as much to be polite as to keep him from hounding me about it. But I had no intention of following up on my shallow promise. Noise, pollution, crowded streets lined with beggars, disease...not my idea of a good time.

That same evening I cycled into Auckland. I had a place to stay with friends I had made while hiking on the South Island. Wendy greeted me at the door with a letter in her hand. It was from Richard and Jill, friends who were on a global bicycle journey on their tandem mountain bike. The letter had arrived in Seattle, been forwarded to my parents in California, and then forwarded to Wendy's address in New Zealand. It had journeyed around the world as well, having been mailed from...India.

After spending a grand evening with Wendy and her friends, I sat propped up against the headboard in her guest room, wishing for something to read. I searched the room and found one book. It was *City of Joy*, the story of a priest who lived in a slum of Calcutta, India.

That was three. Were these signs? Or just coincidences?

I soon forgot the day's events and busied myself with packing for my flight home.

One of the things I love about traveling for any great length of time is, upon your return, a mountain of mail awaits you. Yes, most of it is bills and junk mail, but the sheer mass makes me feel important. I was busy sorting, dividing it into "personal" and "I'll get to it sooner or later," when I came upon an announcement from the airline I had all my frequent flier miles with. I opened it up and sat in open-mouthed silence. The letter proudly announced one new destination...New Delhi.

"What is it?" my brother asked.

"I'm going to India," I stammered.

"Why?"

"I have absolutely no idea."

# Road Warrior

Armed with my sturdy, Indian-made bicycle bell, I attacked Highway 2 south out of Delhi. I felt as if all 8.4 million residents of that city were on the same road: buses, cars, motor-scooters, bicycles, pedestrians, carts pulled by oxen, horses, camels, even an elephant—all dodging and swerving in a vast "car"cophony of noise. The philosophy appears to be, "I Honk—Therefore I Am." Interstate 5 at rush hour is a Sunday stroll in the park in comparison.

There are no vehicle emission standards in India. I'm quite sure I ingested my yearly allowance of diesel exhaust in one afternoon. Huge black clouds of exhaust billowed out of every tail pipe. I rode bandit style with my bandanna covering my nose and mouth; my throat sore within the hour.

I have learned the most important rule of the road: the bigger vehicle *always* has the right of way. This puts bicycles at the very bottom of the vehicle caste system. When two trucks converge, and you, the lowly cyclist, happen to be present, you have but one option other than death—head for the ditch! Time and time again, that's exactly what I did on the road to Agra. And I thought being a bicycle courier in Seattle was exciting.

So I've survived my first encounter with India and relax in the much more serene grounds of the Taj Mahal. There should be less traffic as I head west into the desert region of Rajasthan. Greetings to all with my parting words of advice: Carpool Seattle. Carpool!

# Bicycle circus

There seems to be only one style and make of bicycle in India—a black, single-speed with upright handlebars and fenders. It apparently comes in only one size as well, as I have seen countless Indian boys riding bikes so large that one slip could dash all hopes of ever enjoying sexual intercourse.

The problem this homogeneity poses is that riding a multi-colored, 21-speed mountain bike with bar-ends and panniers is the equivalent of the circus coming to town.

Whenever I pass another cyclist there is the inevitable, "Squeak, squeak, rattle, rattle, clunk" as he speeds up to pass. (I use "he" because I can count on one hand the number of girls I've seen riding bicycles so far.) Once he has successfully passed, wearing a determined grin, he stops pedaling and turns around to get a better look—forcing a radical swerve to avoid collision. This frustrating "leapfrog" can go on for kilometers.

Riding through or stopping in a town multiplies the problem. Just yesterday I stopped at a market and ordered some chai (tea boiled with milk and as much sugar as will hold in solution). First there were five boys and three men observing my mechanical wonder. Then a total of twenty. Then fifty. Within three minutes, a hundred and fifty bodies surrounded me like a human vice, closing in for a better view or a touch. A rather helpless feeling comes over you when that many people collectively invade your personal space. I conquered the urge to scream, paid for my tea, and slowly began to move. And like automatic supermarket doors, the crowd parted.

These situations are ones I am learning to cope with in India and I revel in my "quiet" time between towns in the desert plains of Rajasthan—where the camels could care less *what* kind of bike I'm riding.

# charlie Brown Plays cricket

I was the Charlie Brown of my Little League baseball team. The only time I got on base was when "walked" or "hit-by-a-pitch." I remember other teammate's fathers yelling, "Lean in, Willie. Lean in." My average stood rock solid at .000 and before the last game of the season my manager offered me 10 dollars if I got a hit. The season ended—my manager's net worth remained the same.

In India, baseball does not exist, but its historical predecessor, cricket, reigns supreme. Boys of all ages can be seen playing in school yards, fields, street corners and back alleys.

In the late afternoon, as I pedaled through a small village, I noticed a large group of boys practicing their national sport. They waved me over and one boy yelled, "Do you play?" Before I had a chance to reply, I had a fat cricket bat in my hands and stood in front of the wickets. The tallest boy said, "I throw slow," and prepared with a short run to pitch or "bowl" the ball.

Having observed others playing, I knew to position the bat down by my feet as if I were preparing to hit a golf ball, but the laughter around me confirmed my stance was still unconventional.

The boy tossed the ball and it bounced right. I swung and missed. Over twenty years had passed and my fortune hadn't changed. The boy announced, "Fast now," and smiled. Hadn't I borne enough humiliation? I set down the bat, but a small voice said, "C'mon Willie. Don't think Charlie Brown. Think *Ken Griffey Jr.*"

I picked up the bat and dug in. The boy took a long, running start and hurled the ball with all his 15-year-old might. It bounced and I swung wildly, connecting with a loud "thwack." The ball sailed over the head of the pitcher, over the heads of the boys out in the field, and disappeared behind some large boulders.

Suddenly I was surrounded by cheering boys, jumping up and down and patting me on the back, several of whom were shouting, "Six. Six."

I had just enough knowledge of cricket to know what that meant. It had taken 32 years and a journey halfway around the world—but I had hit a home run.

# camels

After cycling 700 miles to the desert fort town of Jaisalmer, it was time for a break. And what better way to rest the old backside than…to go on a camel safari.

Camels have always been part of my romanticized picture of the desert: camel silhouettes at sunset riding a top massive dunes, the three wise men riding them in search of baby Jesus, Lawrence of Arabia, etc.

Forget it. Camels are the noisiest, smelliest creatures on earth. Dog breath is perfume when compared to camel breath. Their enormous pink bubble gum tongues often hang out of their mouths in a long, low camel raspberry.

Our group of 12 travelers (with Germany, Scotland, Ireland, England, Australia, and the US represented) saddled up our camels and were guided out into the wilderness.

The first day of riding went smoothly and we bedded down for a crystal clear night under the stars. Then it happened. Our camels began to snort and groan and chew and belch and fart as if there was no tomorrow. (I can't imagine the three wise men ever having a serious conversation with these creatures around.) We tried to ignore it, but we were all soon laughing with disgust. We noticed our guides had made their camp upwind of our beasts of burden.

The next morning I was chatting with the head guide and asked what he did before. "Worked in a bus station," came the reply. I said he must prefer working outdoors in the desert. "Are you kidding," he said. "Working with camels stinks." I had no rebuttal.

If I haven't put you off and you would like your very own camel, you can buy a good used one in India for about 10,000 rupees (350 bucks). I forgot to ask if that included the limited warranty.

# A Night in Jail

I was ushered into the police station's holding cell. One chair sat alone in the gray-walled room lit by a shaft of light split by the bars on the only window. This all looked a little too much like my memories of the film *Midnight Express*. "Your passport," said the stoic sergeant and I surrendered it to an armed guard who disappeared around the corner.

Five minutes passed in silence as the sergeant inspected my bike, my gear, my helmet and my water bottles. The armed guard returned with my passport. The sergeant gave it back, smiled and said, "You may stay."

You see—I wasn't a prisoner—I was a guest.

When I arrived in Takhatgarh, Rajasthan, I had no intention of spending the night in jail. But after a group of 50 locals convinced me the only hotel was a den of thieves and drug pushers and personally escorted me to police headquarters, I didn't have much of a choice.

A cot and a television were brought into the room and I was informed the evening's meal would be potatoes with mixed vegetables and rice. I washed up and was served by the smiling in-house cook who filled my plate at the slightest sign of it emptying.

While I was enjoying truly one of the best meals I'd eaten in India, a knock at the door announced the Lieutenant Commander who greeted me and marveled at my bicycle. He then pointed to my sleeping bag spread out on the cot and said, "You demonstrate." I obeyed and climbed inside and zipped up the zipper. He roared with laughter. It was at that moment I realized I was living a stand-up comic's dream: In India, everywhere I went I drew a crowd and everything I did was funny.

Later, as I slept soundly and securely in my cell, a loud rapping came at the bars and I jumped up to a voice calling "English TV, English TV!" I opened the door and one of the guards came bounding in and switched on the light and the TV at full volume. My eyes finally focused on an old black and white episode of Charles Dickens' *Great Expectations* with a young Michael York as Pip. The guard pulled up a chair and smiled, fully convinced I was delighted at this 1AM discovery.

I forced a smile—and couldn't help but wonder if the thieves and drug pushers across town were sound asleep.

# The Bhagvati Binge

I met Bhagvati in an ice cream shop in Banswara, Madhya Pradesh, and he invited me to spend the night at his home. A small, frail man with more-salt-than-pepper hair and a smile that revealed missing and tobacco-stained teeth. After 35 years he had retired from the railway service. He showed me the chair he'd occupied for three and a half decades, earning a top salary of 2000 rupees a month (about 65 dollars).

That evening we walked the streets and stopped at the city park where several food vendors were set up around the perimeter of a large fountain. Bhagvati took me on a tour of Indian fried foods, sampling the dishes at each stall. And although I was the rich American, it was apparent from the start I would not be allowed to spend one rupee while his guest.

He asked which was my favorite dish and ordered a large plate—chick peas in a spicy sauce. While contemplating how I was ever going to finish, he mentioned we'd be eating supper at the home of his dear friends, owners of the local sweet shop. Supper? I thought I was *eating* supper.

Thirty minutes later, with my stomach already at Thanksgiving full-ness, I was served a large vegetarian thali. This plate of food looked more insurmountable than any mountain pass I'd ever climbed. I dug in with mock enthusiasm and chewed and swallowed and smiled. Then Bhagvati dropped the bomb. He leaned over and whispered, "You must finish that and ask for more or they will be offended." I was stunned and began to sweat, not from the spice, but from gastronomical fear. But via a small miracle, I finished my plate and a second helping and sighed, my stomach as tight as a snare drum. Victory was mine.

Then our hostess entered with a platter. Sweets! I'd forgotten the sweets. The livelihood of this family and the ultimate insult if I refused. Couldn't Bhagvati explain I'd like a large box…to go? I picked a creme-colored chunk, as dense as Christmas fudge, and imagined it as light and airy as cotton candy. My taste buds had ceased to function, but I praised it as "food of the Gods" and managed to slip the last piece to the family dog, to whom I owe my life.

After six weeks of cycling in India, the question no longer appears to be whether I'll survive the dangers and diseases…but whether I'll survive the hospitality.

# I Am God

It had been one of those days—hot and dusty, with trucks and buses honking, and a couple of flat tires to top it off. I had stopped on the side of the road to look at my map and get my bearings, when a teenage boy rode up on his scooter and asked, "One minute of your time?" A harmless request, but I have learned in a country of 900 million people, if you give everyone a minute who asks for one, you soon run out of minutes.

In this particular situation I chose to withhold my 60 seconds of attention and pedaled off. Soon came the whine of a scooter as the boy pulled up along side of me. "One minute of your time?" "Ignore him and he'll go away," I thought and picked up my pace. He caught up and began repeating, "Sir, I am talking," over and over and over again. This went on for five minutes and I imagined with my luck, he had a full tank of gas.

I slammed on my brakes. "OK, you win," I said, "You've got one minute," pointing to my watch, "Go."

He looked me straight in the eye and said, "I am God." I was speechless. What is the proper response when a 13-year-old boy confides in you that he is a deity? "I am God!" he repeated more emphatically. What did he want? Did he want me to kneel at his feet? To sing his praises? Did he want my Visa card? "I AM GOD!" I turned to go. "Sir, I am talking. Sir, I am talking."

I snapped. I lost my cool. I became unglued. I yelled at the top of my lungs, "Get out of my face. Leave me alone"…and several other choice phrases.

He took one step back, held out his hand and said, "One hundred rupees."

He must have seen the look of homicide in my eyes, for he quickly hopped on his scooter and scooted off before I could begin to holler again. Thank Krishna *that* was over.

A mile down the dusty highway I began to laugh. I laughed until tears came to my eyes as I realized what the poor kid had meant to say was, "I am guide" and his fee was 100 rupees.

Now I'm not sure where he would have led me, but I'd gladly give a hundred rupees to hear *his* version of the story.

# Back Roads and Back Waters

A bicycle is freedom when you're riding it; it's a millstone when you're not.

With my bike on my shoulder, I waded into the river. In front of me trudged Avadhut, a 17-year-old boy, and his friend with my panniers perched on their heads. This is what happens when you attempt to navigate the back roads to Ratnagiri using a map of Southern India (which is the equivalent of trying to locate Pike Street with a map of the entire Northwest).

Once across the river, all I had to do was push and/or carry my bike four kilometers along a footpath over the hills to a fishing village, where, if I was lucky, I could catch a ferry to another village where the road began again. All this was represented by a single unbroken line on my map. I cursed the cartographer.

Avadhut agreed to be my guide and after snacks and tea at his mother's, we set off on our mini-adventure. We walked under groves of coconut, mango and cashew trees occupied by monkeys and hornbills while discussing Hindi films and Michael Jackson. We stopped at a 500-year-old temple in the forest where priests fed us pieces of coconut from the alter and blessed my bicycle. We shared a melted chocolate bar and a bottle of warm water. We joked with a group of tribal women out chopping and collecting firewood. We took a shortcut, a goat path actually, and how we got my gear-laden bicycle to the top of the hill without ropes is beyond me.

Five hours later, we arrived at the fishing village, bathed in sweat, filthy and full of scrapes and bruises. After a two hour wait, I said good-bye to my new friend and boarded the ferry. (A ferry as defined in India is any vessel that floats and can carry more than one person.) The only other passenger was an old peasant woman unsuccessfully trying to patch together a torn five-rupee note with her saliva. The old diesel engine chugged loudly, but I looked up as I heard Avadhut call out one last time. A thought flashed through my mind—how much more of India would I experience if I got rid of my maps altogether?

# Beached in Goa

The state of Goa is known throughout the world for its beautiful beaches and inexpensive beer—and for the first time in my travels in India, I felt hostility. The people staring at me all had scowls on their faces and foreign passports in their pockets. They were Europeans who had found their beach paradise and were obviously reluctant to share it with anyone. The few people who would speak to me had two things in common—they were in India because it was cheap and they disliked Indians. "They never stop staring," said one man. I suggested this might be due to the fact he was naked and half of his head was shaved. He didn't respond.

I cycled south in search of a friendlier beach and found one. As I arrived, twelve men surrounded me, all asking if I needed a room. Huge packs of screaming children ran amok selling the daily newspaper for twice its listed price, and an intimate crowd of 300 stood on the sandy shore to watch the sunset. A bit too friendly. The next morning I again cycled south.

That evening I sat in a small outdoor restaurant and looked out at the fishing boats as they returned with full nets. I had found my beach: a cove nestled between rocky hills with a small population of locals and travelers. A cool Arabian sea breeze blew, the palm trees swayed and I imagined a beautiful French or Swiss woman joining me for dinner and later walking hand-in-hand under a starlit night. Then reality hit me in the form of a very large, bearded, drunken Englishman who collapsed into the empty chair at my table. "You look like you could use some company," he slurred. There was nowhere to run—all the other tables were occupied. My potentially romantic evening was spent listening to this man belt out Cat Stevens and Bread tunes in a three-note range that would have one believe Joe Cocker was opera trained.

I paid for my fish masala and studied my map. It was time to head inland. The beach scene was depressing me.

# Ear cleaners

"Wanted: Professional Roving Ear Cleaner." Now there's an ad you won't find in the classifieds. These dedicated individuals roam the city streets, preaching the evils of earwax and practicing their art on anyone who sits down and, well...lends them an ear. I didn't believe this job existed myself until there on the streets of Bombay sat eight men on park benches—smoking, reading the daily newspaper and...having their ears cleaned.

I was approached by one the other day as I stopped to fill my water bottles—a soft spoken man carrying a little black case filled with large cotton swabs and dangerous looking metal scoops and picks. "I am a professional and very gentle. See." He handed me a very tattered, somewhat laminated certificate and smiled. It was written in Hindi, but I imagined it stated he had graduated with honors from an accredited ear cleaning academy.

"No charge. I give you free inspection," he said and motioned me to sit on the ground next to a fruit stall. I pondered. I had been cycling the dusty, dirty roads of India for over two months. Why not? I sat.

He knelt down beside me and took out a small flash light and searched. After some hems and haws came the diagnosis. "It is very bad. You have much wax build up. For a very small fee I can remove it. But you have another very serious problem. You have stones in your ears. For a charge of only 75 rupees per stone I will remove them. In a hospital you will pay much more."

With all this excess wax, maybe I hadn't heard him correctly. "Stones?" "Yes," he said and pulled out a large pair of metal tweezers. "Don't worry. I'm a professional." The thought of him accidently removing my eardrum propelled me onto my bike and down the street in seconds. I turned to see him frantically motioning me back while calling out, "50 rupees. 50 rupees per stone."

I escaped what appeared to be a con job, but just in case I'll have my doctor take a long hard look when I get back to the States.

"Wanted: Slightly Used Denture Salesman." I kid you not. But that's another story.

# *Climb Every Mountain*

The sign at the foot of the Nilgiri Hills in Tamil Nadu had read: "This road contains several hairpin bends and steep gradients. You will have to strain your vehicle much."

My vehicle showed no signs of stress. I, on the other hand, was a virtual cycling fountain as sweat dripped from the end of my nose, my chin, my elbows and my fingertips. At one point the road was so steep that for 45 agonizing minutes I was forced to stand while pedaling. (They called these hills—the summit was at 7,000 ft.) I found myself panting out camp tunes from my childhood to take my mind off my aching legs and the 36 switchbacks.

As I struggled with hairpin #22 and my sanity, a passenger in a slowly passing truck called out, "Why you not take the bus?" On the verge of tears I screamed, "I don't know!"

Another eternal half hour passed with no summit in sight and I battled with the thought to give up. It would be so easy to get off my bike and wait for a ride. Then I began to hear the sounds of drums and instruments and through a clearing in the trees I saw a village perched on the side of the hill. They were celebrating the annual festival of the local god, Kalliamma. With new found strength I sprinted to the top.

Smiling faces and laughter greeted me and I was whisked off my bicycle to participate in a large circular dance. Women in brightly colored saris and men in traditional dhotis whirled around me. Two of the men grabbed my hands and coached me through the steps. The local Brahmin priest walked up and gave me a big hug and the villagers cheered. I couldn't help but feel like I'd been plunked down in the middle of a National Geographic special. My tutors must have seen my shaking legs begin to buckle, because they led me off to sit on the grass and brought me bananas and coconut to eat.

Surrounded by giggling children, I looked out at the valley below (the home of wild elephants and tigers) where I had begun my climb. A grin filled as much with exhaustion as exhilaration spread across my face as I once again knew what I have always known—the answer to why I didn't take the bus.

# The Five Questions

What is your name? What is your country? What is your job? Are you alone? Are you married?

I have cycled over 5,000 kilometers in India and been asked this series of questions as many times. The sheer repetition of answering can be a mind-numbing experience. On any given day, after fifty-some-odd inquiries, I begin to get creative to avoid boring myself to death. I become Hans, a professional speed skater from Austria. Or Bernardo, an elevator mechanic from Italy. Or Biff, a talent scout from Los Angeles.

These false statements don't eat at my conscience, for most of the people asking them are more concerned about practicing the few phrases of English they know than listening to the answers. I must admit though, one very bright boy caught me with my cycling shorts down when he asked if I was a speed skater, why wasn't I at the Winter Olympics?

Adults are more likely to continue on to the more personal questions. "Are you alone?" is often miss-phrased as, "Are you lonely?" This poses a problem—for if I answer correctly, "No," they then want to meet the other members of my party, but if I answer "Yes," I send a little message to my subconscious that I am depressed.

Finally comes, "Are you married?" I can't win with this one either. If I answer truthfully, "No," it is immediately followed by, "How old are you?" When this is divulged, looks of genuine sorrow and pity come over the questioners' faces, since in the villages of India, I am long passed the age of any hope of marriage. When I answer "Yes," the response is often confusion or outright offense that I would willingly leave my wife for such a long period of time.

Unless I'm extremely rude and ignore everyone, the question-and-answer game will continue for the remainder of my travels.

So an old, over-the-hill, lonely cyclist sends his love…and any available women out there interested in an arranged marriage can contact my mother for my qualifications.

# *Arnold*

In Batalagundu, a mid-sized town like many other mid-sized towns in India, with bus stand, market, coffee and tea stalls, hotels, assorted cluttered shops, beggars, etc—I took a walk before sunset to snap some photos. While attempting to focus on a holy cow lounging in the middle of an intersection, oblivious to the dodging buses and auto rickshaws, I noticed a boy following me. After clicking my bovine portrait I walked on, but could see out of the corner of my eye that the boy was trying to get my attention. I stopped and he cautiously approached and asked in a barely audible whisper, "Excuse me, sir. Do you know Arnold?" "I'm sorry I don't," I replied. "I'm just visiting here." A look of shock spread over his face. "But you must know Arnold?"

Lets see…the only Arnold I knew of was…nah…it couldn't be *that* Arnold. This was Southern India.

The boy motioned for me to follow and he walked up the steps to his house. As I stepped inside the humble abode, his older sister ran giggling into the cubbyhole of a kitchen.

The main living room contained some small statues of Hindu gods and a large calendar with the electric blue portrait of Krishna. But by far the largest image in the room was a huge poster of Terminator II. It *was* that Arnold. The boy presented his cinematic shrine with pride and introduced me to his mother who ordered her youngest son to round up some tea.

An awkward silence followed as the three of us sat beneath "The Terminator" sipping tea and smiling at each other. "I have tried to write to him," the boy finally blurted out, "but he does not write back. I think he is very busy. Do you think you could deliver a message to him for me?" I tried to explain that my chances for an audience with the Lord God Arnold were not much better than his own.

The boy tried to hide it, but I could read the disappointment on his face. The awkward silence returned, broken only by the giggling sister collecting tea cups. Using the excuse that it would be hard to find my way back to my lodge in the dark, I made my escape.

I waived good-bye to the boy as he stood in the doorway, clutching his Terminator II cassette...the best evidence I've seen to date that the world is rapidly turning into one big video store.

# The Magic Word

Beyond the locked gate lay a road I desperately wanted to cycle; the highest in Southern India, crossing from Tamil Nadu to Kerela through national forest land. The sign written in Tamil and English stated the road was closed to all vehicles. The frowning guard informed me my only option was to obtain permission from the regional director.

I knew the scenario. Back to Kodaikanal, where I would sit in a dank and dreary office for a day or two, only to be told the person I needed to see was away on business and could I please come back in a week.

There was one other option...try some magic. In a similar situation, long ago, Ali Baba used the magic words "open sesame," but that was a different place and a different century, so I softly spoke the word "backsheesh."

The magic worked—the guard's face opened up into a smile, the gate opened up for me to pass, and my wallet opened up to produce 20 rupees. The guard pocketed the bribe...I mean "tip"...and waved me through.

That night I slept underneath Leo and Orion on a cliff overlooking the aptly named "Silent Valley" and for the first time in India I was truly alone. It was glorious. Rising with the sun, I set off after a breakfast of two bananas and a chocolate bar. The dirt road, pockmarked from annual monsoons and littered with rocks the size of softballs, wound up and down the pine and eucalyptus covered mountains. It was more like riding a jackhammer than a bicycle and I stopped near some cabins on the shore of a lake to rest my legs and my wrists.

A man in a green uniform came running up and demanded to see my permit. I gathered I was in serious trouble from his reaction to my lack of one. I was ordered to report to the Chief Warden immediately. A wave of anxiety broke over me. Would I be fined? or jailed? or both? Why hadn't I taken the National Highway?

As I approached the office, walking my bike, my fears suddenly melted away as I remembered the *magic word*. All would be well. I entered smiling and reached for my wallet.

# Bent into Shape

Laying in a semiconscious state in an expanding pool of my own sweat, I stared at the sky and wondered if my body would ever respond to stimulus again. Muscles I never knew I had ached and quivered. My condition had absolutely nothing to do with cycling; in fact, my bicycle had remained locked up for days.

Before my visit to the ashram in Southern Kerela, my knowledge of yoga consisted of browsing through manuals with photos of people bent into positions that looked downright frightening. Was the human body really meant to perform like Gumby? Yet here I was in India attempting (without much success) the cobra, the locust, the plow and the wheel. These positions as interpreted by my body, could be renamed the pain, the torture, the agony and the defeat.

The days were full at the ashram and the structured schedule left very little free time. Squeezed in between 5:30AM and 10PM were four hours of yoga (or asanas), three hours of meditation and chanting, two hours of lecture, one hour of "Karma Yoga" (otherwise known as chores), two meals and two tea breaks. It all had the feel of summer camp, including a pristine lake for swimming (watch for crocodiles) and a corner cafe outside the ashram where you could often find desperate yogis sneaking a smoke or indulging in a large fruit salad.

The head swami, our lecturer and spiritual guide, was a Harvard-schooled Italian who had given up a career in International Law to wear orange and pursue inner peace. His large protruding belly announced one of two things—he had given up on yoga asanas years ago, or he had a secret stash of cheese and chocolate in his room. I agreed with many of the concepts and ideas he shared and found some of his insights quite inspirational. But I must admit, I find it difficult to embrace a philosophy that suggests one abstain from both sex and garlic.

The peaceful surroundings, the healthy food and the chance to exercise without sitting on a bicycle seat were a welcomed break. After my week's stay, I don't feel any closer to true spiritual enlightenment…but I *can* touch my toes.

# The Himsagar Express

While sitting on the southernmost tip of India, watching locals dog-paddle in the combined waters of the Indian Ocean, the Arabian Sea and the Bay of Bengal, I pondered a problem. It had become too hot to continue cycling in the South. Fourteen liters of water had been converted to sweat during the day's ride and I often felt I was melting into the pavement. The solution? Go north, young man, way north.

I had already booked and boarded the Himsagar *Express* before I discovered it wasn't. My journey north would wind up taking 75 hours, the so-called "express" stopping at every *other* station.

As the train chugged along the Kerela coast, I found out why I was surrounded not only by people in the second class sleeper, but by bags, boxes and trunks as well. "Only a fool would check anything of value onto an Indian train," someone said. This fool tried to conceal a claim check for his bicycle.

Winding through Tamil Nadu, I came to the conclusion that Indian-style toilets, which already pose a challenge to Westerners, become downright dangerous on a moving train.

I watched as litter flew like confetti on the plains of Madhya Pradesh, thanks to India Railway's money-saving measure of not providing trash cans.

In Haryana, I learned never to stray far from the platform, as the train unexpectedly pulled away and caught me dining at a snack stand. I made the train, but arrived back at my seat wearing half my dinner.

I conversed with a Sikh while the wheat fields of Punjab blew by. His answer to all of India's problems? Get rid of the Muslims.

As we crossed the border into Jammu, a Muslim, having finished his evening prayers, confided in me, "You can never trust a Sikh, not one of them." So much for Gandhi's philosophy of tolerance.

Throughout the journey the scenery, the weather, the people and the food changed. But one thing remained constant in every state, at any hour and any station: the loud and nasal dronings of the chai sellers, the tea-hawking mascots of the rail system.

After three days, three hours and 33 chais, my bicycle and I arrived in Jammu-Tawi as a cool rain fell. I'm back in the saddle again.

# A Shepherd's Life For Me

A typical Himachal Pradesh traffic jam clogs the mountain highway for miles. Not a vehicle in sight, just a thousand goats and sheep eating anything green in their path while being driven to the market town of Chamba by their shepherds. A shop owner storms out shaking his fist and cursing. A small battalion of goats has laid siege to his vegetable garden and taken no prisoners. A heated exchange takes place between shop owner and shepherds while this weary cyclist sips tea on the sidelines and enjoys, for once, not being the center of attention.

I have quickly fallen in love with this rugged state, shrouded in the beauty of the Himalayas and sprinkled with families of nomadic shepherds with their pillbox woolen caps and wide grins. Now there's an ideal profession: work outdoors, travel, low stress and all the free sweaters you can knit.

The other night as darkness fell with no town in sight, I pedaled up to a group of shepherds camped by a river and asked, in a combination of sign language and very poor Hindi, if I could share their campsite.

Moments later I was sitting by a fire as an old woman with a face carved by years of sun, wind and cold served me a huge plate of rice and dahl. Maybe if I was lucky, they'd let me travel with them for a day.

The last grain of rice eaten, the last dish scrubbed with sand and rinsed; one-by-one they excused themselves and bedded down. Where was everyone going? The night was young. No camp fire songs? Charades anyone?

Disappointed and wide awake I mazed my way through scores of snoozing goats to my sleeping bag. One young boy, who knew some English, walked over and whispered, "Don't afraid. We with you."

The sky was still black when I woke with a start. They were gone. Only dying embers and goat droppings remained. Up the valley I spied flashlights beaming and heard whistles and vocal proddings as they moved on towards Chamba.

I glanced at my watch…4AM! After mentally crossing off "shepherd" from my list of future professions, I pulled my sleeping bag up over my head and went back to sleep.

# Jalori Pass

My heart pounded wildly as the black car with its flashing red light disappeared around the bend along with several other official looking vehicles. It had nearly run me off the road.

This hardly seems worth a mention, as being run off the road can be a daily occurrence in India and I have come to fondly think of the ditch as my second home. But this time there was no ditch, just a 500-foot dropoff to the river below. And as guard rails have yet to become fashionable in Himachel Pradesh, if I had traveled three more feet, these words would not have been written.

I coaxed my heart back down under a hundred beats a minute, tried to whistle a happy tune and continued on towards Jalori Pass.

Jalori Pass had been on my mind for over a week now. It didn't exist on one of my maps and local opinion was running 90/10 in favor of it being closed due to snow (if it did exist). But I had to try. Not just because it was there or because the summit was over 10,000 feet, but because the alternative was to backtrack 100 kilometers and take a flatter, hotter, more boring route back to Delhi.

The muddy road climbed steeply through small villages where I often heard the muffled trampings of snot-nosed Indian and Tibetan school kids as they ran after me in their oversized rubber boots, laughing and giggling. At times I could barely muster up enough speed to keep my bike upright and all sense of athletic achievement disappeared when a 70-year-old woman passed me as she walked with a large stack of wood on her head. "Oh yeah, just wait till the downhill, granny."

Twelve kilometers from the summit, I found a man who could definitively answer my question—a trekking guide. "Sure it's open," he said, "but only for two days now. The Chief Minister decided to take a trip and they cleared the pass for him. He came through today. Did you see him?"...Yeah, I'd seen him.

So it is the chief minister I have to thank for my opportunity to conquer Jalori Pass. And if I see him in the capitol of Shimla, I'll gladly shake his hand...right after I knee his driver in the groin.

# conned

He was so smooth, such a pro, that the money was out of my wallet and I was walking down the street before I had an inkling I'd been had.

As I remember, his first words were, "It's hot today, isn't it?" His soft-spoken demeanor stood out amongst the hoards of street hawkers and beggars. He owned a fruit export business and proudly supplied mangos and papayas to the U.S. Embassy. The spring in his step, he said, was due to his daughter's marriage, the following day, to an American from Berkeley. He offered to buy me a cup of coffee. He wanted to hear more about my bicycle journey.

As the sweet, brown brew arrived, he asked if I would honor his family and be a guest at the wedding. (This didn't seem so strange, as I had been invited to more than one wedding on my journey.) Also, he and his wife were going to see the renowned sitarist, Ravi Shankar, that evening and if I gave him the money to buy a ticket, he'd get me a front row seat. The next day, I would be a guest at their home outside of Delhi, and, if I didn't mind, and he'd like to present as a gift to my mother a cookbook his wife had written…and on and on and on. He was so charming and so believable that I forked over 800 rupees (25 dollars) without thinking.

As I walked down the street the questions began to surface: Why had he written his name and address on a slip of paper? Every businessman, no matter how small, has a business card. Why, if he was as wealthy as his business eluded, did he ask me for money to buy a concert ticket and a small, traditional gift for his daughter?

I began to feel really stupid. But this guy was so good I wasn't certain I'd been ripped off until I'd waited hours at the YMCA for he and his wife to pick me up.

There is a temptation not to write this down at all and never admit publicly that I had been taken, duped, fooled, had. But come to think of it, it was a pretty cheap lesson overall. The price could have been $250...or my bicycle.

What have I learned? Well, not to give money to a stranger on the spur of the moment. I know that! Everyone knows that. But isn't that the art and challenge of "the con"—to get someone to do something willingly that they know damn well they shouldn't do? If only I had told him I didn't have any money with me and I'd pay him that evening. But if I had been thinking that clearly, I would have seen through his lies and leaned over the table and said, "Sir. I'm on to you. How about if you pay me 800 rupees not to turn you in to the police." At least that's what I'd do in the movie version. In real life though, I'm a little embarrassed...but also a little wiser.

# Back to Delhi

Cycling 112 miles the last day, I was like a horse who sensed the barn. A noisy, crowded, polluted barn, but one just the same. After five months and 5,000 miles, the insane traffic of Delhi didn't phase me. I was a veteran, dodging buses and auto rickshaws with the best of them, all while constantly ringing my bell to alert the jaywalking cows and pedestrians. I arrived at the YMCA tourist hostel exhausted, but with a warm sense of closure.

Sitting in the dining room, I spied brand new travel guides perched on tables next to well-scrubbed travelers-to-be. I felt like a soldier, back from the front lines, watching new recruits preparing to leave. Their faces etched with fear and anxiety. And like an old war veteran, I spilled out stories and advice, requested or not. "Now that reminds me of an experience I had in Rajasthan…"

Back in my room, the fan attempting to whir away the 95 degree heat, I imagined waking up at 3AM and opening the door to a cold haze of December—all of it a dusty dream.

So much to process. So much to remember. So many events that have subtly changed me. I don't *feel* changed or enlightened. The only things friends back home will notice are a few more gray hairs and a few more wrinkles (should have used more sunscreen). The other changes will crop up slowly, but they're there.

Many people have commented on how brave or crazy I was to cycle India alone. But I have long since learned to avoid being impressed with my own achievements. Consider a French cyclist I met on the way to Agra. He had already cycled 22,000 miles on his trip, surviving an accident in Malaysia that left him with two broken legs. He was on his way to Bombay to catch a flight to South Africa from where he planned to cycle all the way back to France. Oh, one more little detail…he was 68 years old!

Now I'm not sure I'll be able to accomplish such a feat when I'm that age, but I do plan to continue traveling and observing the world. And until someone convinces me there's a better way...I'll do so from a bicycle seat. Hope you enjoyed the ride.

# South Africa

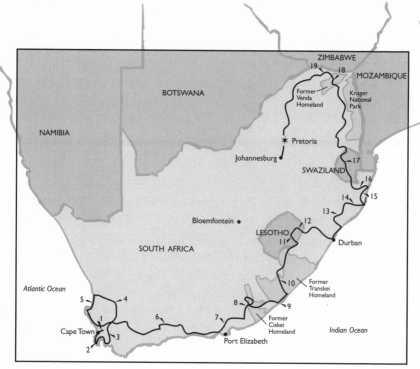

Bicycle Route ——

March 1995 — August 1995

## Map Key

1 – First Flat—First Impressions
2 – The Good Doctor
3 – Beauties and the Beast
4 – Another Day, Another Hill
5 – Flamingo Silhouettes
6 – Carnivore
7 – I Don't Wanna Grow Up
8 – Fear
9 – Shortcut—Long Haul
10 – The Entertainer

11 – The Mountain Kingdom
12 – Lesotho II
13 – Seatless
14 – Another Saturday Night
15 – Rugby Fever
16 – Ultimate Chewy Toy
17 – Swaziland Cowboy
18 – Video Night in Venda
19 – Dr. Travel and Mr. Home

My South Africa journey was the result of a survey and a song.

While in India I met fellow travelers from all over the planet. India rarely attracts the two week vacation tourist. When you meet a foreigner with a tattered backpack and leather skin it is more appropriate to ask how many years they've been traveling than weeks. To these veterans of wanderlust I posed a simple question, "If you could return to one country you have visited, which would it be?"

South Africa won hands down. Some sighted the beauty, others the people and wildlife, but most couldn't give a specific reason. The country simply cried out to them.

This struck a chord with me. A year prior, my friend Laurie had taken me to a Johnny Clegg concert in Seattle for my birthday. Johnny is a white South African who grew up speaking and singing in Zulu as well as English. He and his band, Savuka, put on a concert that to his day echoes in my mind. Half way through, the audience rose to dance and sing and never sat back down. As Johnny sang about South African skies, I swore that I'd see them myself one day.

After I had purchased a one-way, nonrefundable plane ticket the warnings began. The U.S. State Department, guidebooks and most of the people I talked to, advised against traveling in the former homelands or in the townships. It didn't seem to matter that the rule of Apartheid had ended and Nelson Mandela was now president following the first free elections. I was told I'd be safe only if I stuck to the well-worn tourist routes.

I told concerned friends and family I would heed these warnings, but deep down I knew my travels would take me beyond the secure boundaries...and into the South Africa that Johnny had sung about.

# First Flat—First Impressions

My front tire hissed at me, and I quickly felt metal grinding on pavement. Only six kilometers into my South Africa bicycle journey and I had my first flat. The pessimist in me immediately projected ahead. "Let's see…," I thought to myself, "one puncture every six kilometers, divided by the total distance I've planned for this trip, means I can look forward to fixing 1,676 punctures." I leaned my bike against a railing on the No. 2 national highway leading from the airport to Cape Town and began the repair.

Cape Town is considered by many to be the most beautiful city in the world, but lift up its outskirts and you'll find the Cape Flats—a sprawling township composed of endless rows of tin and scrap wood shacks, thickly spread across a dusty, treeless plain. It was in the midst of that crushing sprawl that flat No. 1 occurred.

As I dug for my repair kit, a tour bus stopped alongside. This bus had windows so large I could tell what brands of shoes the passengers were wearing. "I don't mean to sound paranoid," the driver yelled. "But you should get a ride into town. Strange things happen on this road, if you know what I mean." I gave the driver a "thanks-but-no-thanks" look and he returned it with a "fine-with-me, it's-your-funeral" shrug.

Seconds after the tour bus pulled away, two black men emerged from the bushes and walked slowly toward me. "Great," I thought. "Thirty-seven minutes into my journey and I'm going to be robbed." I was a 21-speed rolling K-Mart: camera, dozens of rolls of film, binoculars, tape recorder, tent, sleeping bag, stove, tools, spare parts, and some cash—a thief's Blue Light Special.

As the men approached, I hit my target heart rate without moving a muscle. Not wanting to look up, I focused on my tire pump and the task at hand, expecting at any moment a knife to appear, or for one of the men to jump me. They stopped two feet away. I tried to whistle something light-hearted, but only managed to drool on myself. I finally glanced up. The two men smiled, and then walked away.

I breathed a sigh of relief, and with it came a flood of questions: Was I going to spend the majority of my time in South Africa worrying about being robbed? Would I have reacted the same way if two white men had emerged from the bushes? Why had I so quickly jumped to conclusions?

In the coming weeks, and the months that follow, I will have the opportunity to observe the new South Africa—including its problems, fears and prejudices. But in doing so, I must also face my own.

# The Good Doctor

The doctor forced me to groan and bite my lip, and I cursed him for it. He delighted in my pain and slapped me once again in the face.

I am, of course, speaking of the Cape Doctor, the name locals have given the relentless southeastern wind that blows all the pollution out of Cape Town and vicinity. Pedaling my way to Cape Point Nature Reserve, I didn't need an appointment to meet him. Typically the Cape Doctor is a phenomenon that only occurs during the summer, but had unexpectedly lingered into autumn with a gale-force vengeance, at times making forward progress impossible.

What kept me going was the knowledge that I had a warm bunk awaiting me at the reserve's Environmental Center. A lovely woman I'd met arranged my stay there. I tried to call ahead to reconfirm the room, but the lines had been downed by the doctor.

I was cycling along a dramatic coastline. Below me waves tore at the base of Africa, and above a sheer cliff pushed into the sky. This little pocket of the world sports more plant species per square kilometer than anywhere else on earth, including the rainforest. I reminded myself to look up time and again to enjoy these wonders, but each time I did I received another slap from the doctor.

After hours struggling to keep my loaded bicycle upright, I arrived at a turnoff to the center and stared up at an 18% grade. My legs only functioned because I promised them, this would be it for the day. Rest and a shower awaited.

As I gasped for air at the top, the director greeted me sheepishly. Something was wrong. "You must be the cyclist," he began with the obvious, and after a few hems and haws, "I'm terribly sorry, but we are completely booked up with a scout troop and I can't allow you to stay." I responded politely that I understood. My legs wept.

I sat beside my bicycle, dejected, nursing a water bottle. It would be 23 kilometers to the nearest campground, and the sun was setting. A boy approached and said, "I talked with my scout leader and asked if she could make an exception. She told me she wasn't keen on having a strange man staying about."

Strange man, indeed! Didn't she know a bicycle was the internationally recognized symbol of the forthright, honest, and trusted traveler? Obviously not. I waved to a group of boys as I rolled back down the hill. This unfortunate group of scouts would have to forgo my skillful demonstration of the one knot I know how to tie.

I am presently bedded down for the night in the dirt and scrub, huddled beside a large bush that protects me from the ever-howling doctor. A little gray mongoose is staring at me and protesting my intrusion. I'll gladly put up with his insults as there are four species of venomous snakes to be found in this park, including the Cape Cobra. Pleasant dreams.

# Beauties and the Beast

Light, airy music played as tea cups clinked saucers set on flowery table linens. Cloth napkins blossomed out of tall, crystal wine glasses. Seated for tea time at "Le Petit Ferme," with views of lush green vineyards, were the loveliest ladies of the Franshhoek Valley, dressed in fine attire and speaking softly in Afrikaans.

Driven down from the mountains to seek shelter from a raging thunderstorm, I sat, a beast among beauties, wearing the dirty polar fleece top I'd used as a pillow the night before while camped in the woods beside the highway. My cycling shorts dripped next to soggy shoes. Road grime clung to my unshaven face and the hairs of my legs. My perfume? "Ode de Road."

As a cyclist I try to avoid places with cute French names. These inevitably are *dining* establishments. Touring cyclists seldom dine, they feed. The goal is quantity, not cuisine.

I perused (and dripped on) the menu: "Rainbow trout de-boned and succulently hot-smoked—a specialty," and miles beyond my budget. Where was the cyclists' menu? "Healthy portions of peanut butter, tenderly wrapped in bread of wheat." Or, "Chocolate-chip cookies, de-boxed, and served with four liters of chilled nectar of bovine." My decision quickly narrowed down to the one thing I could afford: tea and scones.

When my order arrived, I wasted little time appreciating the artistically arranged platter, and summed up the situation. If I cut each of the two scones into three pieces instead of in half, thus creating more surface area on which to pile all of the jam, butter, honey, and whipped cream provided, I could attain maximum consumption without resorting to directly spooning condiments into my mouth.

Moments before I attacked my plate, a plaque hanging on the wall next to me caught my eye. It read:

*A day in such serene enjoyment spent*
*Is worth an age of splendid discontent*
*Eat slowly; only men in rags and gluttons old in sin*
*Mistake themselves for carpet bags and tumble victuals in.*

At first I smiled at staring patrons as I daintily scooped hundreds of calories' worth of sugar into my tea, making sure I held my pinkie high as I sipped. I gently wiped the corners of my mouth with my serviette after each jaw-stretching mouthful of condiment-laden scone. But soon the beast in me emerged, and I chomped and slurped and shoveled.

My feeding frenzy was interrupted by the exit of the four women seated at the table next to mine. I grunted farewell, wiping away misguided whipped cream from around my mouth with the back of my wrist. An eerie stillness came over Le Petit Ferme as the beast, waiting to pounce, spied his next prey on the abandoned table—a perfect, untouched scone.

# Another Day, Another Hill

"You're the first bicycle tourist I've seen on this road since we bought this farm," the man said, leaning on a spade on the edge of a tilled field.

"When was that?" I asked, wiping road dust from my teeth with a bandana.

"Let's see," he began to figure. "That would be 1968."

The road through the Cederberg Mountains came highly recommended by several locals. It wound through a wilderness area with towering slab peaks, once the home of the Sans bushmen, made popular by the movie *The Gods Must Be Crazy*. What the locals forgot to mention was this road was so rugged and steep that few of them would ever consider driving their own vehicles over it, let alone a bicycle.

My farm stop had a dual purpose; to ask for water and to stall, for beyond the plowed field was one of the steepest hills I'd ever laid eyes on. The farmer must have seen my lip quiver as I gazed at the cruel incline. "I can baakie you to the top, if you'd like," he said, referring to the back of his four-wheel-drive pickup.

Years ago, at the age of 19, I would have immediately declined. The mere thought of accepting a ride was tantamount to defeat. Fifteen years later, I thought long and hard, with the words "Yes, please," poised on my lips. But my vocal chords malfunctioned and an inner voice confirmed, "Accept a ride today, Willie, and tomorrow you'll be touring South Africa in a big tourist bus with your bicycle stowed in the luggage compartment."

In place of a ride, I did accept a bag of dried fruit with his parting words, "You'll need the energy."

Shifting into first gear, I positioned myself in the middle of the road for the climb. (There was no need to worry about traffic; I'd seen one vehicle in the past 24 hours.) As I grunted and strained, a small blue fly played hide-and-seek in my nostrils and ear canals, while my rear wheel fishtailed, searching for traction. I could manage only 200 to 300 meters before my legs felt as if they'd combust, and then I'd stop and pant and check my heart rate, hovering at 210. At one point I gave up riding and began pushing my bicycle up the hill, but instantly found out that it was depressing and more difficult than pedaling. So it was back in the saddle, where I composed scathing letters to each and everyone who'd suggested this route.

At the top of the hill my adrenaline took over and I cheered. I yahooed. I would have yodeled if I knew how. "No baakies or busses for me!"

My celebration lasted only long enough for me to wipe the stinging sweat from my eyes. From my victorious perch, the road descended sharply and there, across a tiny valley, lay another hill, the mirror image of the one I'd just conquered. In humble silence, I stuffed a dried pear into my mouth and began the slow, rocky descent. My day had just begun.

# Flamingo Silhouettes

There was no doubt in my mind. The moment I saw them a little boy's giggle escaped through my smile. Five seconds I'll never forget. A travel memory created.

At Elands Bay, on the west coast of the Cape, I shared a campsite with Suzi and Annie, two women who had spent the last 17 months wandering through Africa. Their tattered tent barely stood up to the afternoon gusts of sand-spitting wind, and mine nearly tumbled away before I could stake it down.

While we were planning yet another low-budget traveler's meal of pasta and S.O.S. (something on sale), our neighbors peeked over our wind-shielding hedge and invited us for dinner. We jumped at the opportunity, not only for the food and company, but for a look at their tent. This family from Pretoria had been coming to the same campground for 30 years. Their Barnum & Bailey-sized tent engulfed the entire site. I kept expecting a family of Lithuanian gymnasts to stroll out each morning.

The inside was palatial: large, thick mattresses, a dining table, stove, sink, and full-sized refrigerator. Fishing nets had been wetted and stretched to create a sandless floor.

We stuffed ourselves silly on barbecued snook (a popular local fish), wine, and bread topped with homemade jam. An evening of South African hospitality, including hugs and kisses good-night.

As we walked out of "Circus-Circus" and back to our humble domes, I heard muffled honking, and turned, expecting to see geese. I grabbed Suzi's arm as I saw the unmistakable silhouettes of three flamingos with their gravity-defying necks and long legs stretched, smoothly gliding across the moonlit waves.

My memory raced back three decades and I was holding my mother's arm while pushing the turnstile at the Sacramento Zoo. The day's goal was, of course, the monkey house and the bears. But first, always first, was a stop at the big concrete pool hosting the flamingos. "The zookeepers must paint these birds," I remember thinking. "Nothing is this color naturally— except cotton candy." I got down on my hands and knees and looked up, making sure the few standing on single legs weren't amputees. And I wondered what they'd look like if they could fly—not old enough to understand their wings had been clipped. Then it was off to the monkeys, dragging my mother by her left arm, which to this day is two inches longer than her right.

That little boy never imagined that one day he'd see those amazing creatures while cycling in a distant country. The man he became is still giggling for it. I've now seen flocks of hundreds feeding in multicolored lagoons, but I'll always treasure that moonlit sighting.

Travel's lasting memories seldom come from destinations planned. They are found in fleeting moments and flamingo silhouettes.

# carnivore

Vegetarians beware! South Africa is a land of meat eaters; a carnival for carnivores; a land where butcher shops outnumber video stores; where— sing to the tune of the last lines of "Home on the Range"—seldom is heard of bean sprouts and curd, and your arteries harden each day.

I have eaten more meat in the last month than I had in the previous decade. This on-slaughter of animal flesh began even before I "touched down" with a raw bacon sandwich served as a snack on my flight to Cape Town (three fatty slices on a bun with a paper-thin slice of tomato as garnish). I thought there had been some mistake until I witnessed another passenger, a high-school student returning home from a skating competition in the Netherlands, gobble his down without hesitation. The poor kid looked so hungry...I gave him mine.

In South Africa, a meal isn't a meal without meat, and an event isn't an event without a braai (pronounced "bry"), or barbecue. At every corner store you can purchase beef pies, liver pies, mutton pies and game pies (a pie stuffed with something you've seen on *Wild Kingdom*.) In the region called the "Little Karoo," you can dine on an ostrich burger and enjoy dried beef sticks the size of your leg.

I can avoid the cholesterol loading when preparing my own meals (although I did discover that the second ingredient in the soya pasta mix I fancied was beef fat), as there is always peanut butter and bread.

The real problem lies in the hospitality of the locals. I am often treated as if I were the prodigal son returning home, and the fatted calf is quickly slaughtered (or at least defrosted). In one household I was treated to the family favorite—beef and liver casserole. I learned in a college nutrition course that your body takes hours, sometimes days, to digest meat. This is fine if you have a leisurely afternoon planned, but I often embark on six to eight hours of activity minutes after eating a meal.

One morning last week I was invited in for breakfast at the farm where I had been allowed to pitch my tent. The two sons were eating large bowls of oatmeal with brown sugar, raisins, and fresh milk. Perfect. The youngest was in the process of ladling out my portion when his father entered, slapped his hand, and announced, "He'll have none of that. He has a mountain pass to climb on that bike of his. He needs a proper breakfast." Out came sausage patties, followed by bacon and eggs, all fried to stomach-seizing perfection. I watched longingly as the leftover oatmeal was fed to the chickens.

Despite the physical ramifications, I will continue to be polite and eat what I am served while cycling South Africa.

For your information, I'll be taking an extended break from my journey sometime in July. I'm scheduled for a triple bypass.

# I Don't Wanna Grow Up

Had my ears deceived me? The pickup truck ahead of me moved slowly up the unpaved road, but I heard no engine. Was it electric, or simply tuned to perfection? I pedaled hard, passed, and immediately had my answer—the vehicle ran on *grass,* not gas. The owner had sheared off the front of the truck at the cab and replaced the motor with two donkeys, harnessed and struggling in first gear; a brilliant solution to high petrol prices, as long as he didn't mind shoveling exhaust in the city.

I continued on and pulled into a small store in the equally small town of Addo. The place teemed with people due to the holiday weekend, the anniversary of national elections and the launching of the new South Africa with Nelson Mandela at the helm.

Conversations buzzed around me as I packed provisions into my front panniers. But I could only enjoy the laughter, and the tones and clicks, for everyone spoke Xhosa (the "xh" is pronounced as a click). Soon after having stuffed an entire loaf of bread into a space the size of a tennis ball, I looked up to see five men surrounding me. One inquired in English about my bicycle. I answered the "How much? How far? How long?" trio of questions, and then asked one of my own.

"I have noticed a couple of young men dressed in Western suits with their faces painted a dull orange... What does this signify?" Instantly eyes looked away, feet shuffled, and hands dug into pockets. It was as if I'd vanished and the men spoke among themselves in Xhosa.

"Wrong question?" I thought to myself. Had I offended them? Should I apologize? Or should I simply get on my bike and ride away?

I turned slowly and reached for my handlebars. The tallest man stepped forward. "It is part of our black culture," he said. "When a boy wants to become a man he must..." There was a long pause, and a few of his friends snickered. "He must..." He shifted his weight from side to side and glanced up at the sky. Then he repeated a vertical chopping motion in the air with his right hand. His friends turned away and I spied shoulders quivering. "He must have his…" The chopping hand moved down toward his belt.

Bingo! "He must be circumcised," I blurted with game-show enthusiasm.

"Yes," the man sighed, with a grateful grin, as his friends burst into laughter.

The man further explained that the initiation was performed in the bush, with no painkillers and (one hopes) a very, very sharp knife. It was not uncommon for the individual to die from infection. This step into adulthood was the boy's own choice and only occurred when he decided it was time to become a man.

I thanked the man for tackling the extremely sensitive subject, and we shook hands.

"What is your name?" he asked.

I grinned…"Peter Pan."

# *Fear*

"Do you want to die?" The short, stocky farmer grabbed me by the shoulders and his eyes locked onto mine. "If you take this route you've planned to King Williams Town, you'll be killed. Don't you understand? I know these people. The Blacks…"

His voice suddenly dropped to a desperate whisper. Standing around us were his workers, all of whom were black. "The Blacks are a different breed from you and me. Life means nothing to them. They'll kill you for that watch on your wrist. You must change your plans and go up into the Orange Free State. Here, I'll show you."

He grabbed my map and traced a route along the major highways clear to Johannesburg. It was a perfect route—for a trucker.

I thanked him for his advice, but said I'd prefer to continue along my chosen route. "You're a fool, soon to be a statistic." He walked away.

Fear. Like a sour brussel sprout, is an unwanted part of my daily South African diet, a diet otherwise rich in kindness, hospitality, and natural beauty. In the eight weeks I've cycled here, I can't think of one experience, one moment even, when I've had a good reason to be afraid. But every single day I'm reminded that I *should* be afraid. I'm constantly being offered advice: which roads to take and not to take, where not to camp, which parts of the country to avoid, to always carry a gun, to never travel alone—all of which relate to fearing people with darker skin than my own. As I ride along, I find myself balancing between caution and fear: Caution keeps you *aware*. Fear keeps you *away*.

I'm not one who thrives on danger. At Disneyland at the age of five I crouched in terror at the bottom of the boat throughout the "Pirates of the Caribbean" because a friend had told me one of the pirates fired live ammunition. Of course, no bullet ever grazed my skin, but the suggestion that one might was enough to keep me at the bottom of that boat.

South Africa is not Disneyland. Real bullets are fired here as they are in every country on our not-so-peaceful planet. In the two days I spent in King Williams Town, which lies on the border of the former homeland of Ciskei, four people died in an ongoing taxi war. (Taxis aren't regulated in this city, and when too many vehicles glut the market, competitors often begin shooting at one another.) This, of course, is the only news South Africans will read about King Williams Town.

However, while I was there I discovered a community filled with incredibly friendly people. I was even given the opportunity to speak at a local primary school that only five years ago was only for whites. Of the group I spoke to, half were black. The headmaster was ecstatic that I'd come. "We don't get many travelers or foreigners visiting. It is even hard to fill teaching positions. People are afraid. Hopefully time will change that."

I'm presently headed toward the Transkei (another area I've been warned hundreds of times to avoid). I often think of the racist farmer's comments. Perhaps I am foolish, but if the alternative is to become imprisoned by fear, I'll gladly remain a bicycling fool.

# Shortcut—Long Haul

There is no bridge over the River Kai. No road hugs the ocean along South Africa's aptly named Wild Coast. Inaccessibility has preserved its pristine beaches and abundant bird and marine life. For example, the distance between Kai Mouth and Wavecrest is a mere 20 kilometers as the crowned crane flies. But by car you must drive 75 axle-breaking kilometers along dirt tracks, or over 120 kilometers on teeth-shattering roads.

Two men seated on off-road motorcycles shared the small ferry as we crossed the great Kai River. Both of them assured me my best route would be the coastal one. "Take the shortcut," one man yelled as he revved his unmuffled engine. "On a bicycle you should have no problem reaching Wavecrest by nightfall."

With a low spring tide, the sand on the beach was hard as a smooth asphalt road and I effortlessly cycled along it. Fish eagles soared across cloudless skies and a school of three dozen dolphins played in the surf. "Forget nightfall," I thought to myself, "I'll be in Wavecrest by lunch."

That dream road abruptly ended as the sand turned soft. It swallowed my front tire, and nearly pitched me over the handlebars. I pushed for a while, then pulled, then dragged my bike through it. With the now incoming tide, my sandy beach quickly disappeared and I had to time the waves in order to slip past huge rock walls. One wave caught me unaware and drenched me from cap to sandals.

One hour and one kilometer later I found myself struggling up a steep sand dune. At the top was a small cottage. I was greeted at the door by "Knuckles," an old man with a sun-wrinkled face. His two remaining front teeth held fast his stub of a cigarette. I showed him my map and asked about crossing the Kobonqaba River.

"Let me put it this way," he grinned, "with the tide in, you could stand on my shoulders and we'd both drown. You'd better stay here and push on in the morning."

I was wet, upset, and annoyed. "Shortcut," indeed. I swore never to take advice from someone on a motorized vehicle again. Then I glanced around and for the first time noticed the view from Knuckles' porch—the rugged coastline stretched out forever, an ellipse of blue that ebbed and flowed across miles of beach. I laughed at myself. Why was I in such a hurry? Wavecrest was just a place on a map. I had no reservations, no appointments, no pressing schedule to meet there.

I accepted Knuckles' offer and was treated to a glorious sunset while a full moon simultaneously rose over the Indian Ocean. We swapped stories and swilled coffee late into the night.

The next day at low tide I waded across the Kobonqaba River three times—twice with gear, and another with my bicycle above my head. I arrived at Wavecrest a full day later than planned. My shortcut had turned into a long haul, and it no longer bothered me in the least.

# The Entertainer

A gust of wind sent clouds of dust and plastic bags whirling against tin shacks and gutted cars. Vehicles maneuvered around huge potholes on the unpaved highway, and clusters of people wrapped in winter blankets shuffled about as I pedaled up to a roadside store. I waved a friendly greeting—the only smile in return hung 20 feet in the air on a billboard announcing a new and improved laundry soap. "Gets even fatty stains out," the woman beamed.

This area was filled with "naughty boys," or so I was warned by Milton, my 78-year-old host, who had allowed me to camp on his property the night before. What did he mean by naughty?

"They'll slit your throat," came his matter-of-fact reply. That sort of activity scored at least an "8" on my personal naughty scale. I promised Milton I'd be careful.

The store personnel glared as I perused the half-empty shelves, selecting a carton of long-life milk and two oranges. As I searched my pockets for money, I noticed a crowd begin to gather. Three tough-looking men blocked the path to my bicycle. I peeled an orange and felt very foreign, and very alone.

A few minutes passed and I came to the realization that the next move in this stand-off was mine. The three men slowly stepped aside as I approached my bike. I reached into the pocket of one of my panniers and felt for the only security measure I had for this type of situation. I spun quickly around to face the crowd and began tossing bean bags in the air.

I learned to juggle in high school while on the tennis team. As the last alternate on the "B" squad, I spent most of my time sitting courtside, and as there are three tennis balls to a can, this skill developed out of sheer boredom.

My impromptu South African performance would not have secured me a job with Barnum & Bailey, but it was executed with enthusiasm and conviction: the Lazy Man's Juggle, the Helicopter, behind my back and under my legs. For my finale I threw one bag high in the air, crouched at the last second, and caught it in the nape of my neck. Then, with a quick whiplash snap, I sent it skyward, and caught it in my baseball cap.

The crowd, which had tripled in size, cheered and clapped. The tension had melted away and I faced a crowd full of smiles and grins. The three formerly menacing gentlemen patted me on the shoulders and asked me where I was from and where I was going.

After an encore performance I cycled out of town. I glanced over my shoulder and watched the waving crowd disappear in a cloud of dust and plastic, ever so thankful I'd never mastered the game of tennis.

# The Mountain Kingdom

The glassy-eyed border official pushed the stamp down firmly on the inkpad and then smacked it onto my open passport. Nothing. It was too cold for the ink to stick. He breathed alcohol-soaked breath on the stamp in an attempt to warm it up and then tried again. Nothing. Finally, with the help of a cigarette lighter, he managed to produce a barely intelligible, upside-down entrance stamp in my passport. Welcome to Lesotho—the Mountain Kingdom.

My first concern as I crossed the border was shelter. The sun was sinking as fast as the temperature, and at 8000 feet, I knew I'd spend a frigid, sleepless night in my flimsy tent. But where? The barren road ahead wandered through barren mountains.

An hour later, with a tightly woven Basotho blanket wrapped around my shoulders, I stood outside a hut in the tiny village of Hamonyane. Several children, oblivious to the cold, danced around me in their underwear. I didn't know how to say, "Are you crazy? Get some clothes on," in Sotho, so I remained silent, watching the sun set behind an awesome curtain of jagged peaks. As the darkness crept up the deep river gorge, I became aware of a thousand stars in the sky—and a million goosebumps on my bare legs. Friendly voices called me in for supper.

I was the guest of Joseas. We'd met on the side of the road and, after he convinced the chief of the village I was not in search of a wife, permission to stay overnight was granted. Joseas is a grandfather at 39. His kind face has been spared the lines and wrinkles one would expect from the hard life of the gold mines. There is no work in Lesotho, so for twenty years he has traveled to the mines in neighboring South Africa: twelve months of mining followed by 56 days' leave. Only 56 days to visit his family and home.

We sat down to a dinner of sheep's heart, lung, and intestine, prepared over a cow-dung fire by his wife and mother-in-law. As the honored guest, I was awarded the largest slabs of fat. I managed to smile while my stomach turned somersaults.

As we got ready for bed, children's voices could be heard singing from a neighboring hut. I asked Joseas what the song meant. "The lyrics talk of how the rest of the world sees Lesotho as a tiny kingdom. But we think it is big because it is rich in mountains, water, and cattle." I fell asleep under three heavy blankets and the spell of the magical melody.

The next morning, after six and a half cups of tea, we hiked down into a gorge. Our conversations echoed back as Joseas led me through the caves where shepherd boys sheltered the sheep and cattle during heavy winter storms.

"How many days left in your leave?" my question bounced all around us.

"Thirty-three," Joseas sighed.

Back at the village, a squadron of nine boys and three dogs waited to guide me back to the road. Joseas and I shook hands, then embraced.

"I hope a time comes soon when you can watch the seasons change in your own country," I said. "But for now I wish you 33 more splendid days in the mountain kingdom you call home."

Joseas smiled and wiped away a tear. I turned and began pushing my bike up the path.

# Lesotho II

The old Basotho woman beckoned me into the large hut with a gesture and a smile. I hesitated, but she grabbed my hand and led me inside. I stumbled blindly, like a late patron entering a darkened theater. My ears heard music and laughter. My nose smelled wood smoke and pungent sweat. My skin sensed bodies swaying and twirling. My eyes saw nothing.

I had entered a shebeen, a local drinking and dancing establishment, and I'd lost hold of my elderly date. With my hands outstretched, to protect my face from any large, solid objects, I made my way slowly toward the music. Live or recorded? I couldn't tell. My hands made contact with flesh. There was a yelp and all percussion ceased. I had my answer. I'd nearly thumbed the drummer in the eye.

Light flooded the shebeen as someone opened the door and many patrons became aware for the first time that there was a foreigner amongst them.

I apologized to the drummer. His one, waist-high drum was made of sheepskin stretched over a cylindrical wooden frame. Several pieces of metal, strung through coat-hanger wire, were positioned so he could hit them on both the up and down strokes, for a muffled cymbal effect. I shook hands with the other half of the band, the squeeze-box player.

A strong hand grabbed my shoulder and spun me around. An old tin can was thrust at me, and all eyes watched as I accepted it. I wasn't sure whether to drink the contents or ceremoniously sprinkle it over my head and feet. Then it dawned on me. This one was "on the house," and I took a hesitant sip. The crowd laughed at my facial reaction to the lukewarm, bitterly sour, gritty liquid.

Then the band struck up again. My dance card became full. Everyone, male and female alike, wanted to boogie with the American. My dance partners all had Lesotho's harsh mountain climate etched on their faces, but here it was warm, and all blankets and concerns had been checked at the door.

After buying a round for the band, I reemerged squinty-eyed and rubbery-legged into what remained of a winter's day. My progress had been painfully slow in Lesotho; I'd struggled to cycle 150 kilometers in five days along the rugged mountain roads.

A car hauling a trailer pulled up as I pushed my bike back onto the road. Familiar accents spilled through the windows—fellow Americans. They had driven the entire length of Lesotho on the main highway in one day. They spoke of the vistas I'd missed and some roadside parks, then quickly rolled up their windows and zoomed off toward the South African border.

I shook my head, not the least bit envious. It was true, they had seen more of Lesotho in a single day…but I had experienced more of Lesotho in a single hut.

# *Seatless* (*Nowhere Near Seattle*)

I will admit, as I'm sure will thousands of others, to an ongoing love affair with the bicycle. It has been my constant companion over 50,000 kilometers of travel. I have yet to meet anyone, though, who will sing praises of the bicycle seat. Far from it. The most hated of bicycle parts, it makes life miserable—rubbing, chafing, bruising. It is, in layman's terms, a royal pain in the butt. I have often wished I could cycle without sitting on one. Last week my wish came true.

It was a cloudless day in Kwa Zulu Natal. I had camped the previous night with some archeologists at a remote dig on the banks of the Tugela River. As I pedaled, my mind brimming with stories of the prehistoric inhabitants of Zululand. Suddenly, with a sharp crack, my seat pitched forward. On inspection, I discovered the two bolts holding the seat to the post had snapped. Not a problem. I reached for my tools. They weren't there. Big problem. Had I lost them or had they become part of the South African wealth redistribution program? Lost or stolen, it didn't matter. They were gone.

I looked around at the brown hills dotted with brown huts. The odds of finding a six millimeter allen wrench were slim.

There I stood performing a touring cyclist's Shakespeare. I pondered my detached bicycle seat held high in one hand, as did Hamlet with the skull of his friend Yorrick, and with dramatic flair I proclaimed, "Alas, poor saddle. I knew it well."

No one applauded my soliloquy. Two white-chested ravens, my only audience, cawed their disapproval. It was time to get this tragicomedy on the road. So, for the next 25 kilometers of hilly gravel roads, I stood and pedaled.

As I panted and grunted, I couldn't decide whether the local Zulu tribes-people were laughing because I was a foreigner on a bicycle or because

I was a foreigner on a bicycle without a seat. A couple of times my memory lapsed and I habitually sat down, only to be painfully reminded that my once-cursed friend was missing.

My arms, my legs, my neck, and my back ached after hours of what can only be described as the stair-climber workout from hell. Finally, I came upon a roadside repair station, temporarily set up to maintain construction vehicles. The necessary tools were found and I bolted my seat back to its rightful place. After tea with the head mechanic, I was on my way again.

The road climbed steadily, rising high above the Tugela Valley. After 10 kilometers I reached the summit and began the long, slow descent. And with glorious pleasure…I sat. Unlike Hamlet's buddy, my friend had been resurrected, and I vowed never to take him for granted again.

# Another Saturday Night

Tired of the same old Saturday night routine—going to the theater, out for dinner and a movie, staying home and watching a video? Ready for a change? How about spending the night camped out on the floor of the Tip-Top Auto Garage outside of Ulundi, South Africa, sheltering from thunder showers? Sound intriguing? Then you may be ready for the life of a long-distance bicycle traveler.

Yes, I had other options. For instance, I could have stayed at the Holiday Inn in Ulundi, where my room would have been clean and sterile, the staff apolitical, and the only lasting memory…a readout on my credit-card statement.

But I chose the Tip-Top. The owner, Joseph, waved as I pedaled up, and I asked him if I could pitch a tent nearby. He offered his hand in greeting and his garage for cover. Other "guests" had preceded me as the repair station had no door. I cleared a place for my sleeping bag amongst goat droppings and nesting chickens.

A couple of locals stood in the corner swigging beer from tall, liter bottles and talking politics. Holding a huge mug of sweet, brown coffee brewed for me by Jerico, one of Joseph's wives, I joined in the discussion. I only had to ask one question. "What do you think of President Mandela?" (Ulundi is the headquarters of the Inkatha Freedom Party [IFP]—the bitter and sometimes violent rival to Mandela's ANC.)

I never spoke another word. Curses flew and beer dribbled on unwiped chins. Predictions of chaos, secession, and civil war were accompanied by waving arms and stamping feet. Accusations mounted as bottles emptied.

Enough of politics. It was time for some entertainment. Joseph and his family and friends had never seen a tent before, so I bet Joseph I could set mine up in under five minutes. The crowd watched in wonder and then cheered as my free-standing dome stood functional in 2 minutes, 42 seconds. (My personal best is 1 minute, 34 seconds while under siege by black flies in Northern Canada.)

Throughout the evening troubled motorists would wander into the garage, assume I was the owner (due to my white skin) and go into lengthy explanations in Zulu of car or mini-bus problems. I'd shake my head and point to my sleeping bag as if to say, "I only sleep here," and Joseph would laugh and come to the rescue.

It grew late and neighbors and other onlookers finally left. Joseph asked his son to go to their house next door and get me a drink. The little boy appeared five  minutes later, walking ever so slowly, his eyes transfixed by the glass. Laughter filled the garage. The boy had filled a 10-oz. glass to the absolute brim with whiskey. I only joined in *after* it had been made clear I wasn't required to drink it all.

One-by-one family members excused themselves. "Good night, Willie. Good night, traveler. Good night, white man."

Joseph was last. "Good night, my friend."

I wrote in my journal and then blew out the candle, falling asleep to the sound of clucking chickens and rain dancing on the tin roof.

Another Saturday night on the road.

# Rugby Fever

It was the day South Africa stood still. From Cape Town to Jo'burg life was put on hold while in pubs, stores, and homes, the masses watched the big event. Super Bowl Sunday paled in comparison. It was closer in magnitude to watching Neil Armstrong walk on the moon. The Springboks had made it to the finals and were playing New Zealand to decide the winner of the World Cup of Rugby.

I witnessed the spectacle crushed between 75 other beer-drinking, biltong-chewing fans at the rugby club in Hluhluwe (lisp twice and you've pronounced it correctly). I say "other fans" for I too was one.

When I arrived in South Africa I didn't know the difference between a scrum and a try. But I soon learned, for the country had a collective case of rugby fever. Every product endorsed it. Every newscast covered it, and every conversation got around to it. Infection was inevitable.

It began when I delayed my trip to Lesotho by a day to watch the opening match against Australia, a game South Africa was expected to lose. But they didn't, and the fever set in.

In the coming weeks I cycled hours out of my way to watch South Africa advance. I was now in Hluhluwe thanks to Andre and Alan, two big-bellied fisherman who gave me a lift from the TV-less False Bay Nature Reserve.

South Africa had been barred from the first two World Cups due to apartheid. Few South Africans ever dreamed they'd witness a black President wearing a Springbok cap and jersey, greet players on the field, or that they'd see a colored man (Chester Williams) star in the traditionally all-white sport.

Regulation time ended with the score tied and, for the first time in rugby history, a game went into overtime. Our barkeep went into overdrive. The volume of excitement began to rise at the Hluhluwe club—

a dull roar of feet stomping and hands slapping table tops, punctuated with groans for missed kicks and cheers for defensive tackles. South Africa scored, bringing everyone to their feet. With two minutes remaining the roar dwindled to silence as everyone stared at the screen and prayed for the clock to run out. The barkeep even stopped pouring.

The tension broke as the official blew his whistle. The game was over. South Africa had won. The crowd erupted and the walls shook from cheers, yells, laughter, and singing. I found myself hugging burly men I'd never met and dancing silly jigs with my fingers in my ears to prevent permanent hearing loss.

After twenty minutes of unrelenting celebration I noticed a woman sitting in the corner with a sombre look on her face. I approached and asked with a shout why she looked so sad. Had she been rooting for New Zealand?

"No," she replied, lifting up a small South African flag on a stick.

"Then why the long face?"

"It's over."

"Yes, but you won."

"You don't understand. Now that the World Cup is over … it's back to talking politics."

# ultimate chewy Toy

A man dressed in khakis and shouldering a rifle put up his hand, signaling me to stop. Behind him were two tribal women with baskets balanced on their heads. "Do you know there are lions here?" he asked. "Yes," I said. "Are you not afraid?" "Not really," I replied without much conviction. The man shook his head slowly in disbelief and walked on, trailed by the two women.

This exchange took place in the middle of a corridor road which ran through a private nature reserve. The man with the gun was paid to escort locals along the four kilometer stretch that connected two public roads. I had no idea this service was available. When I arrived at the entrance to the reserve no one was manning the gate. A picture sign warned of wild animals and another showed a hungry lion growling at two strolling stick figures. The figures had a big red circle around them with a slash through it—the international symbol for "no walking on the wild side."

What was I to do? The noon-day sun beat down with a vengeance and I hadn't spied a vehicle for hours. Backtracking and going around the reserve would take an extra day. Tired and frustrated, I reasoned that since there was no sign prohibiting bicycles, I wouldn't be breaking any rules…and it was only four kilometers.

The road was straight and flat, running through open savanna. The surroundings were exactly the same as I'd been riding through for days, but the possibility of lions lurking about got both my heart and my adrenaline pumping. I must admit to picking up my pace and scanning every bush after meeting the armed escort. I reached the other gate without incident and thought the locals probably were a little paranoid.

Later on that afternoon I met a game ranger while photographing a half dozen giraffes. "I'd let you bicycle through the reserve," he said, "but you wouldn't last long." "Why?" I enquired. "Riding a bicycle is actually much more dangerous than walking. You see, lions are cats and as you probably know, cats like to chase things. They wouldn't eat you unless they were hungry. They'd just bat you around a bit."

I grew weak in the knees as I realized how stupid I'd been and resolved not to become the ultimate chewy toy for a 700-pound cat.

I explored nature reserves in Natal and the Transvaal, but left my bicycle at the gates, hitching rides with other visitors. At Umfolozi Reserve I saw both white and black rhino, one of the last places on earth where these two species still roam. At Mkuze, hippos snorted and grunted while lounging in a river lined with crocodiles. At Kruger National Park, the largest in South Africa, I watched and listened to a leopard dine on a tortoise, cracking and crunching away. Later that same afternoon I gazed in wonder and then terror as a bull elephant walked up to our vehicle while our driver searched for first gear. Wildebeests, fish eagles, kudu, zebra, jackals…each park brought new sightings and new wonders.

Although I gazed through my binoculars until my eyes ached, never once did I even catch a glimpse of a lion. Considering my lapse of intelligence and reason…I am truly thankful I'm alive to tell you how disappointed I am.

# Swaziland cowboy

I closed my eyes, held my breath, and ducked my head to protect my face from flying gravel. The rainless winter had left Swaziland's unpaved roads bone dry. The truck passed at twice the posted speed limit and my world turned brown as huge clouds of dust mushroomed in every direction. I coughed as the fine, gritty powder settled, sticking to every exposed, sweaty part of my body. This scenario was repeated with every passing vehicle, providing me with a temporary tan and a new nickname—"Topsoil Willie."

In spite of these frequent dustings, I was enjoying Swaziland. It had a laid-back, friendly feel to it. Many of the locals wore brightly colored tribal dress as opposed to the Los Angeles Lakers and Chicago Bulls T-shirts and caps that are the rage in South Africa.

My severely parched throat needed something, anything, cool to drink. It was Sunday and many of the small shops were closed so I pulled into a service station. Once inside, my ears captured a familiar sound, one they had not heard for months. From a small radio in the corner of the snack shop came the unmistakable twangs of a pedal steel guitar.

"Do you like this music?" asked the attendant as he entered the shop. "Radio Swazi plays country-western from 1:00 to 2:00 on Sunday afternoons. I never miss it. But my own collection is nothing but Don Williams."

I ran through the limited list of country artists I knew. "Dwight? Kenny? Dolly? Hank?"

"You can have them all. Don's the best."

I ordered a soft drink.

"I want to go to America," the attendant continued, "to Texas and ride a horse. Cowboy life is the best. Do you want to see something?"

Before I could answer, there was a loud clunk. He had swung his leg up onto the counter, displaying a finely oiled and polished cowboy boot. "Now I can die with my boots on. Just like in the movies. How much for a horse in your country?"

I admitted that I didn't know the going price for a stallion, then asked him his name.

"Bheki."

"Becky?"

"Yes, Bheki."

"Well, Becky. If you ever find yourself deep in the heart of Texas and belly up to a bar, you might consider a name change."

"Why?" he asked, handing me a Pine-Nut soda.

"You may not get the reaction you want when you say, 'Howdy, pardners. My name's Becky.' It just isn't a cowboy name." I avoided bringing up the gender issue.

Bheki swaggered out to the pump to service a police vehicle, his boots not quite matching the yellow and red company cover-alls. More vehicles pulled in and it became apparent our conversation would not continue. I tried to get his attention, but Bheki was busy adding a quart of oil to a logging truck.

I pulled onto the highway and began coasting down a hill when there came a voice calling, "Hey Willie! My name is Bheki, but you can call me Don!"

I gave him a thumbs-up and we exchanged a final wave. It was sad in a cinematic sort of way. The Swaziland Cowboy stood station-bound and it was I who rode off into the sunset.

# Video Night in Venda

Little children ran from me in tears. Old women avoided any eye contact and quickly passed by. Young boys stared at me from behind the safety of a row of bushes. These kinds of reactions can quickly lower one's self esteem. What was I doing? Nothing, other than sitting on the porch of a general store. But I was doing so in Venda, a former homeland in the northeast of South Africa. During apartheid, whites avoided this area and today few tourists stop on their way north to Zimbabwe.

I befriended one of the store workers, Zachariah, who spoke English. It was he who warmed me up to his fellow villagers, telling them it was all right to come closer and then interpreting their questions. The idea that a white man would stop just to visit was hard for them to accept. But after a couple of hours I was playing trucks with the kids and cards with the men.

Afternoon turned into evening and Vincent, the store owner and a bachelor, invited me to be his guest for the night. Our dinner consisted of scrambled eggs, baked beans and miele-pop (cornmeal and water cooked to the consistency of play-dough).

Vincent then cranked up the generator to provide electricity. The room had no furniture, but was equipped with a stereo, color TV and VCR. A group of nine young men arrived filling the room to capacity. I knew my chances of viewing a South African "art" film were anorexically slim. A video was selected and up popped Chuck (that's Norris, not Heston). I have successfully avoided Mr. Norris' films in the U.S., but have been subjected to them in Mexico, Central America, India and now South Africa. I didn't catch the title, but Chuck seemed intent on destroying half of Vietnam.

Vincent decided to listen to some music so he turned off the volume of the TV. This warranted no response from the other viewers. Catching the dialog was not necessary—none of them spoke English, and Chuck breaking necks and machine-gunning battalions translates without the need for subtitles.

Talk about a comic cultural potpourri! There I was, sitting in a village in South Africa, munching on dried mapane worms, watching Chuck Norris blast his way through Vietnam while Dolly Parton sang "9 to 5 (what a way to make a livin')." Simultaneously, singing and chanting could be heard from across the road where several boys were going through initiation ceremonies.

It was too much for me and I began to giggle and then laugh uproariously. Angry glances shot my way. How could I find this funny? Our hero had just been wounded.

Then suddenly, the lights went out and Chuck and Dolly were silenced. It is the only party I've been to that ran out of gas, literally. Chuck's victory would have to wait for another session…there was no more kerosine for the generator.

# Dr. Travel and Mr. Home

"Zimbabwe—26 kilometers." I looked up at the sign and an internal struggle began.

I have a split personality like that of Dr. Jekyll and Mr. Hyde. In my life they go under the names of Dr. Travel and Mr. Home.

Dr. Travel loves everything about the road: strange foods, moonlit campsites, dust and sweat, dog-eared maps leading to who knows where? The aching muscles, the uncertainty, the challenge. New cultures, new friends, new experiences.

Mr. Home longs for the familiar: lattes at Starbucks, baseball games, checking the mailbox, "Where shall we eat? I know where!" The firm mattress, the certainty, the routine. Old favorites, old friends, old times.

Dr. Travel wanted to go on. "Forget the expense!" follow the baobab trees into "Zim" and cycle clear up to Cairo. What did it matter that he had bookings to speak at schools in the fall? They'd understand. Mr. Home was ready to turn around, to cycle to Johannesburg and fly back to the States in time for his nephew's birthday. His clothes were wearing thin and his funds were running out.

I sat by the side of the road and ate an apple with some cheese while my two personalities duked it out. By the time I threw the core out into the bushveld, Mr. Home had won...this time.

Turning my bicycle around I began to pedal to Jo'burg.

I reflected on 4,000 miles of cycling in South Africa. In my handlebar bag was a book filled with addresses of people I'd met along the way. Folks who had fed me and housed me, given me directions, suggestions, and all but adopted me into their families. South Africa had long ceased to be "that place of apartheid" or "the country often mentioned on CNN." It was now a part of me.

My mind pedaled back across mountains, through villages and along gravel roads. Back to a town named Clanwilliam in the Cape where I met Theo and Esme in the town park. They shared their picnic lunch with me and also a part of their lives. They were six and eight years old when uniformed men came and informed their families that their neighborhood had been declared a "Whites Only" area. Their families were given three months to move. They talked of anger and shame and of their life-long struggle for equality.

When we got up to leave Theo said, "You must understand, Willie, five years ago we could not have sat with you in this park. It was for whites only." But this was the "new" South Africa and a white man and a colored man embraced in the park, and for the first time in my life I truly understood the meaning of freedom.

I'm now on a flight to Los Angeles. Mr. Home is ecstatic and will soon be back to familiar surroundings. Maybe my travel days are numbered. Maybe it's time to settle down. Get a job with stability and a pension plan. Who am I trying to kid? Dr. Travel is gazing at the world map in the in-flight magazine…planning, dreaming. It's only a matter of time.

# The Balkans

Bicycle Route ———
Train Route ·······

May 1996 — October 1996

## Map Key

1 — Depressed in Budapest
2 — Veggie Pizza
3 — Cool Reception
4 — You say Slovakia,
   I say Slovenia
5 — Barely Camping
6 — Su and Mosquito
7 — Bilisane
8 — Sleeping with the Enemy
9 — Border Games
10 — Midsummer Night's Dream

11 — The Weight Of Human
   Kindness
12 — The Thief
13 — Sick And Tired
14 — No Forwarding Address
15 — Grandma and Grandpa Bunea
16 — Back To School
17 — Muxi
18 — Razor Burn
19 — Highway Robbery
20 — Heading for Home

"You're insane!" That was probably the most frequent response when I told people I was going to bicycle the Balkans, followed by, "Watch out for mines."

I rarely argued or tried to explain. As soon as people heard "Balkans," they thought "Bosnia." Friends imagined me spending five months dodging bullets and land mines.

It was the region, not the war, that fascinated me. Slovenia with its mountains, Romania with its Gypsies and painted churches, the Black Sea coast, and the rarely explored countries of Macedonia and Albania.

Everything was set. I knew the routine. I would be leaving once again on a 4-5 month solo bicycle journey as I had every year for the past six. My commentary series would once again be heard on public radio station KUOW. I had a new bike provided for me by Rodriguez, new water-proof panniers provided by Ortlieb, and new underwear provided by Mom.

Many people envied my lifestyle—"footloose and fancy free." Through speaking engagements and part-time work I managed to save enough money in seven months to pay for my travels the other five. Not many people get to do what they really love for a living and I was one of them.

But I wasn't happy as the plane lifted off from Seattle's airport bound for Budapest. My heart was not in the adventure ahead. It was back in Seattle, grounded. I had gone and done the one thing a wanderer should never do. I'd fallen in love.

# Depressed in Budapest

Cloudy skies cast a dim light on the busy streets of Budapest, and I was depressed. Professional wanderers aren't supposed to fall in love. This one had.

Four magical months after literally bumping into her at the Highland ice skating rink, I left the woman that my little nephew fondly calls "Kissie Girl" behind in Seattle. In the weeks prior to our tearful departure at the airport, I kept telling myself it wouldn't be so hard. I was wrong.

Other factors added to my darkened mood. On arriving in Amsterdam I was told I "ceased to exist" in the airlines grand computer reservations system, and it might be days before I could fly on to my destination. I spent four hours alternately arguing, demanding, and pleading before I was issued a seat.

At the Budapest Airport my bike box emerged in such a condition that I could only venture two guesses: It had been rolled down several flights of stairs, or the handlers had used it for kick-boxing practice. Now it was beginning to rain. I leaned my bike against a building and took refuge in a phone booth. While the rain turned to heavy showers, I practiced feeling sorry for myself.

I watched as, one by one, umbrellas began to open—yellow, green, red, and blue—each adding a splotch of color to the gray cobblestone street. Laughter wafted into my booth of sorrows as lovers, school kids, lawyers, and shoppers dashed for cover. A fat man waddled by wearing a plastic shopping bag as a temporary helmet. A little boy stomped a puddle up on to his father's slacks. By now there were so many umbrellas open that the corner resembled a giant multi-colored azalea. The air no longer smelled of diesel exhaust but of spring.

A loud rapping startled me and I looked out to see a sopping wet gentleman holding a phone card. I couldn't think of anyone to call locally at the moment, so I emerged from my protective shell, running to my bike. While I was frantically digging for my rain jacket, I realized that for the first time since I had left Seattle I was smiling.

I peddled down the rain soaked boulevard spraying gritty fishtails from my wheels. Suddenly I was ready for a new adventure. New sights, sounds, and people to encounter. But only one thought kept that smile on my face. At the end of my journey, I have a date with Kissie Girl. We are scheduled to meet at noon on September 27th at the Parthenon in Greece.

I'll be there. I promise.

# Veggie Pizza

I scanned down the first three pages of the menu of Restaurant *Da Wally* in Budapest. It was printed in Magyar, the national language of Hungary, so not a single word did I understand. My table companion, a kid from Boston, was having the same problem. We had wandered over from the backpacker's hostel, where the motto appeared to be, "Drink till the bars close, then climb a bridge."

Rob was in the midst of an impassioned expose on how to pick up Hungarian babes when my eyes latched on to a familiar word, "Pizza."

Now I could have ordered fogas or kacsa or even zsemlt, but I had no idea whether they were animal or vegetable, raw or cooked, solid or liquid. I wasn't in the mood for cuisine roulette, so I unadventurously ordered a large veggie pizza.

A half an hour later, my meal arrived topped handsomely with yellow and green bits. Hand picked peppers? Summer squash? Chives? Closer inspection revealed canned corn and canned peas randomly distributed atop lukewarm cheese.

I didn't want to attempt to complain in a language I did not speak and it *was* a veggie pizza after all. The menu hadn't specified what *kinds* of vegetables…and it *was* large.

As I was brought up to do so, I ate the whole soggy disc, using both hands to keep peas and corn from rolling onto my lap.

Sixteen hours later, after my digestive system had managed to sort out the whole sordid affair, I was ready to try again.

While wandering a back street, the clatter of plates and flatware drew me into a dreary, hole-in-the-wall establishment. The tiniest of signs read *Bufe*. This was where the local workers rubbed elbows—literally. There were no tables, only waist-high counters to dine on. The place was packed, a reassuring sign.

The man in front of me kindly informed me of the names of the dishes others were eating as I pointed to them. Suddenly his face lit up and he said, "Goulash. You like Goulash?" "Goulash" was again repeated, but this time from the kitchen. The cook waddled her way up front, smiling. "Goulash. You like?" I nodded yes and her smile widened impossibly further as she clasped her hands to her chest.

Seconds later I stood in front of a steaming bowl of potatoes in a savory broth with large tender pieces of meat spiced with paprika. Large slabs of brown bread were provided for dunking.

As I ate I occasionally glanced over my shoulder and caught the cook proudly watching. I nodded, toasting her with my spoon, held high.

"Hold the veggie pizza, folks," I thought to myself. "I'm in a goulash state of mind."

# Cool Reception

"Colleague!" (Col-EE-gay) the man bellowed as he slapped me on the back and poured me another glass of white wine with a splash of seltzer. I was quickly getting drunk on a humid Sunday afternoon in Dobrovnik, Slovenia, surrounded by men sweating in suits. I would soon need to make a hasty retreat or somehow drastically influence the wine-to-seltzer ratio.

What was the occasion? I had no idea. But it beat the fate of hundreds of sweaty truckers only 10 miles away. The border of Hungary and Slovenia is closed to commercial vehicles on weekends, so a seemingly endless line-up of trucks had stretched for miles. I counted as I cycled passed the big rigs parked on the side of the shadeless highway, losing track at over 400 before crossing into Slovenia.

What I didn't realize is the party had only begun. Ludwik motioned me to leave my bike outside and follow him. He opened the door to the local meeting hall. Cool air, laughter and music spilled out. Several tables were decked with fine linen and piled with meats, cheeses and elegant desserts. White and pink ribbons hung from the concrete ceiling and draped above the 3-piece, electric synthesized band set up on the stage. This wedding party now numbered over a hundred well-dressed guests and one dirty, smelly cyclist.

The band picked up the tempo to a fast polka as I was served a large platter of food. I watched as guests of all ages danced and twirled about the room. More wine and even less seltzer. The volume soared as everyone joined in the singing.

Ludwik sat next to me singing and slapping his knee to the beat, breaking his cadence occasionally to slap me on the back and yell, "Colleague!"

Many of the guests had now made a large circle and were dancing arm-in-arm. Ludwik grabbed me and the two of us joined in. I was thrust between two older women who appeared to find my placement in the circle inappropriate and sent me down the line twixt two younger (probably single) young ladies.

Ludwik's wife grabbed a hat and a cane with ribbons on it and danced a solo in the middle of the circle. Where was all this frivolity at the weddings I'd attended in the U.S.? All I remember is polite reception lines and tasteless white sponge cake.

The feverish dance ended and I was introduced to the bride and groom and the bride's father and mother. (Thank God I was wearing my formal black cycling shorts.)

As Ludwik escorted me outside, I turned and the entire reception party (including the band) stopped what they were doing and waved goodbye in unison. It was right out of *The Sound of Music* (minus Julie Andrews).

Ludwik gave me a kiss on each cheek and a huge bear hug. I was back to pedaling again with one last "Colleague" ringing in my ears.

Bicycles are magic. They open doors. At least for me they have. To homes, huts, and hovels across the world; to fiestas in Mexico, festivals in India, ceremonies in South Africa and now a wedding reception in Slovenia.

Would Ludwik have waved me over if I had been waiting at the bus stop or driving a rental car or simply strolling by? I doubt it. But because I'm riding this gear-laden, human-powered, open-air vehicle, I've been in Slovenia for less than 4 hours and already have a memory to last a lifetime.

# You say Slovakia
# I say Slovenia

## (Let's call the whole thing off)

Large, dark thunder clouds had developed and were depositing their contents in the form of heavy rain. This is generally not a problem for me. The panniers on my bike are 100% waterproof. You could throw my bike in the river and when you fished it out, my stuff would still be dry. But during this 1AM deluge, I wasn't on my bike—I was in my tent.

My tent is approximately 98% waterproof. This 2% leakage translated into a lot of water over the course of the storm. After two hours, the inside of my tent qualified as a wetland.

This is the time when, at 10 years old and camping with friends in your backyard, you dash inside, your mom makes you hot chocolate and you watch a bad science fiction movie on TV. At 34, and camping at the base of the Julian Alps in Slovenia, you gather everything to the driest part of the tent and shiver while waiting for sunrise.

It is amazing how slowly five hours can pass while sitting alone in a cold, wet tent. I tried to focus on warm, sunny thoughts, but only managed to dwell on what mistakes I may have made on my tax return and, "Why hadn't I learned to play the piano?"

Morning came and brought with it sunny skies and clear, crisp views of the Julian Alps. Compared to my previous night's endeavor, cycling up the steep, winding Vrsic (Ver-seech) Pass was a pleasure. The views were too spectacular to dwell on what parts of my body were aching.

At the top there was a small snack stand and a couple of picnic tables. A short, smartly dressed man in his sixties asked me where I was traveling.

"Through the Balkans," I answered.

"But you're in the Alps are you not?" came his swift reply.

"Fair enough. I'm cycling Eastern Europe."

I might as well have slapped him in the face.

"Slovenia is *not* Eastern Europe!" he said tersely. "It is part of the West."

His reaction didn't surprise me. I have observed that Slovenia has an image problem. (Without looking at a current map, could you tell me where it is?) Most people get it confused with Slovakia and the rest don't even know that it exists. In case you're still pondering, Slovenia (once part of the former Yugoslavia) is the Massachusetts-sized country which borders Austria, Croatia, Hungary and Italy. Slovenia only saw nine days of war back in 1991, but its tourist industry is still feeling the negative effects.

I showed the man my guidebook which classified Slovenia as an Eastern European country.

"Your guidebook is wrong."

I tried to explain to him my problem. "You see, I told everyone back home that I was cycling the Balkans, but I began in Hungary which doesn't qualify. And now you tell me that not only am I not in the Balkans, I'm not even in Eastern Europe."

He leaned over and with a grin said, "Why don't you just tell them you are cycling a piece of the world and leave it at that?" We shook hands and departed without further international incident.

So there you have it. My problem solved, I'm continuing to cycle a piece of the world and if I happen to wander into the Balkans and someone agrees to let me call them that, I'll let you know.

# Barely camping

I stared at the bill in disbelief. There was a site fee, a per-person fee, a National tax, tourist tax and a puzzling "first day" tax…all totaling over 60 Kuna (almost eleven dollars) for a small patch of earth on which to pitch my tent, with an odoriferous toilet nearby. I could get a room at an inn for fifteen dollars. This was ridiculous.

Camping on the highly-touristed Croation Islands in the Gulf of Kvarner was getting on my nerves. Peak season was fast approaching and the campgrounds were filling up. This area, having been far from the front lines of the war, was recovering more quickly than the resorts further south. This is where Germany comes on holiday, as evident from all prices being first quoted in Deutchmarks rather than in Kuna, the local currency.

Now I am, without argument, a frugal traveler. Tourist boards do not have me in mind when they print their flashy, high-gloss brochures. When given the option, I'd much prefer bunking in a farmer's hay loft than staying in an organized campground. But when no other option is available, it is my opinion that nowhere on earth should it cost one person more than ten dollars to pitch a tent (even if a free round of mini-golf is included).

There had to be an option. There was. I took my clothes off.

You see, Croatia has a series of nudist campgrounds, distinguished by a sign with the letters "FKK" and by the absence of tan lines. They are secluded (for obvious reasons), well-maintained, clean, and cost 30-40% less than regular campgrounds where shedding your clothes is frowned upon.

While searching for the ferry terminal on the Island of Krk (pronounced "kirk" with a rolled "r"), I happened upon one such establishment. I was a bit reluctant at first, but frugality won out. Besides, this would allow me to live out one of my reoccurring dreams…bicycling naked.

For those who are curious, not everyone was sans clothing. The receptionist was fully clothed. The maintenance-man using the weed-whacker was too. On the tennis court, there was a sportily dressed man playing against a woman in nothing but Nikes. Disrobing was not a requirement, simply the norm.

After pitching my tent, I sauntered on to the beach, determined to blend in with the well-oiled, bronzed crowd. I wondered why I was getting more than my fair share of gazes, until I realized that while my face, arms and legs were tan, the rest of my body was a pasty, Seattle-winter white. My chest reflected the afternoon sun with the efficiency of a well-polished mirror.

But the novelty soon wore off and I was warmly accepted into the camping community. I played some volleyball, watched a flaming red sunset, and for the first time, I washed all of my clothes without having to worry about what to wear while they dried. The only disappointment was that cycling naked is far more uncomfortable in reality than in my dreams.

So I'll leave you with this travel tip: When in need of a campsite while wandering Croatia, look for the "FKK" sign. Not only will you have fewer tan lines, you'll save a few Kuna as well—even after factoring in the cost of extra sunscreen.

# Su and Mosquito

Su looked at me and said, "You're a freak, Seattle-man. I like freaks."

The fully-bearded, barrel-chested Croatian wearing a long sleeve peasant shirt raised his glass and toasted me with what, to my taste, appeared to be pure alcohol. Su was his nickname.

"I didn't like your Mr. Clinton at first, but now I am a big fan." He offered me a large chunk of bread and the slab of meat on the end of his military knife.

I owed this meeting to a tiny winding road I spotted from the ferry that sails from the island of Rab to Croatia's coast. My original plan had been to cycle down the shoreline. But the coastal road was also the main highway. And I have discovered that wide roads lead to destinations. Narrow roads lead to adventures. This road had adventure written all over it—steeply snaking and switch-backing its way up into the Velebit mountains.

It was slow going due to the severe grades and loose gravel. I watched the islands below disappear in the darkness, then reappear in the moonlight. I slept out in the open near the road.

The next morning I reached the top and a hiker's cabin, where I met Su…and Mosquito.

Mosquito was as thin as Su was round. He wore bright yellow and blue shirts, multicolored pants, and strapped to his enormous backpack was an open, bright blue umbrella.

He had hiked and guided others through the Velebits for as long as he could remember. When the war came, he traded his umbrella for a gun. He led missions in the same mountains to destroy Serbian communication systems. His girlfriend had been his training officer.

"Many times, Seattle-man," Mosquito said, "the Serb soldiers were only meters away, but I hid like a rabbit." He smiled and pantomimed the scenario.

After lunch, we all hiked down the road and some locals invited us to sit in the shade for a drink outside their war-damaged home. Everyone knew Mosquito. The man who dresses like a rainbow.

He grabbed a guitar and strummed awhile. Then he played and sang a song he'd written. A "Croatian freedom song" he called it. It told of a man who fled to Italy because of the war and of a conversation he had with the statue of David.

Mosquito and his girlfriend were departing that day to be the first to hike the length of the Velebits since the war ended. "There is evil in the earth now. The Velebits are strewn with mines. But I will always hike these mountains," Mosquito said defiantly.

Su took out of his pack a well-worn forest service map. "You'll need this or you'll get lost." He showed me where to get water and a good place to camp. "Most of the mines are north and you are going south, but don't stray too far off the road."

I offered to pay for the map.

"It is my gift to you, Seattle-man, because you are a freak. The world needs more freaks."

I waved good-bye and pedaled off into the woods, thinking about Su's statement. I took it only as the highest form of compliment.

# Bilisane

The church of Bilisane in the distance was inviting. Its steeple rising far above the trees promised a safe place to camp. On the outskirts of town I passed a car parked on the side of the road. It had no wheels, no windows, and several bullet holes. The first house looked normal, from a distance. Constructed of gray cinder blocks with a red shingled roof. But long, black, sooty streaks led to broken windows and the remnants of fire. I passed more cars and more homes. The same. Only the church appeared unscathed.

I got off my bicycle and gazed around me. Only that morning, a mere 40 kilometers away I had been laughing with Marco, Mierko, and Sonja at their holiday beach cottage on Croatia's coast. Ten kilometers back I'd cycled through Obrovitz and saw signs of the war—several bombed out buildings and many others pockmarked from bullets. But there was activity and its people were rebuilding. Where were the people of Bilisane?

I approached the church through high weeds. An open door to a church is usually inviting. This one was daunting.

The smell of bird droppings and plaster dust greeted me as I stepped inside. There were no pews or benches left. A wooden desk sat askew in one corner. Every drawer had been wrenched open and what remained of the contents lay strewn on the floor. Some of the paintings had been ripped or removed from the walls. An iron candelabra hung from the ceiling, its candle holders bent or detached. Only a makeshift lectern, draped in an orange tapestry embroidered with a cross, looked in place, as if someone had returned and gently placed it so.

Bits of broken glass and plaster crunched and popped beneath my feet as I walked about. My heart skipped a beat as I startled a pigeon and it escaped through broken windows.

I stood in the middle of the sanctuary, uneasy and afraid. In the 30 minutes I'd been in Bilisane I had not heard a sound other than crickets and birds. No Cars. No dogs barking. No kids playing. It was my ears, not my eyes that finally pronounced Bilisane dead.

I broke the eerie silence in the only way that seemed appropriate. I sang a couple of verses of a hymn I learned as a child. I'd always loved the way your voice echoes in a church. Now it only made me want to cry. I pitched my tent in the nearby woods and tried to fall asleep, listening to the birds and crickets…and nothing more.

My next day's journey brought more of the same. Kastel Zegarski, Ervenik and every other town and village were deserted—every house burned and gutted. All this contrasted by green fields sprinkled with red poppies and cherry trees full of fruit.

My water bottles were empty, so I cycled to Kistanje, a larger dot on my map. I arrived to find wider streets, larger buildings, and the same destruction. A strange sound caught my attention and I looked down the long boulevard. The image will never leave me. There amongst gutted buildings, rubble and glass, an old woman, dressed all in black, was sweeping a section of the sidewalk outside of what I assumed was once her home. I asked if there was water. She indicated there was none and continued her sweeping. Her small section of sidewalk was perfectly clean.

Fortunately for me, I ran into some U.N. troops later on, and they filled my water bottles. They informed me the area I'd come through was heavily mined and hoped I hadn't strayed from the road. The towns and villages had been occupied by ethnic Serbs who fled or were killed during the August Croatian offensive.

The people of Bilisane would not be returning. Others would eventually move there and another town would rise in its place. Bilisane had ceased to exist. It would only be remembered in the hearts of those who had lived there and forever etched in the memory of a weary cyclist who stopped for the night.

# Sleeping with the Enemy

Clad only in my cycling shorts, I stood hunched over soaping up my hair. Five feet away an old woman with a garden hose waited for her cue. I motioned and she sprayed the icy water. Her target was my head, but her aim being far from perfect, she first hit my leg, then my shoulder. This caused me to squeal, her to laugh and our audience to howl. Soon I was completely drenched.

Our audience consisted of three families all living together in a small house off the highway between Mostar and Sarajevo. It is a beautiful road, winding through river canyons. But there are no hotels or campgrounds. All have been abandoned or demolished. IFOR tanks and supply trucks outnumber civilian vehicles and one must slowly cross temporary one-lane pontoon bridges erected next to the twisted wreckage of bridges destroyed.

I had managed to explain my situation in sign language to two men working in a vegetable garden. They gave me permission to set up my tent near their home. I had almost completed the task when a woman came running over yelling and waving her arms. The same woman who now held the hose. She pointed at the tent and I made the assumption I'd soon be departing.

But her anger turned toward the two men. She helped me pack up my tent, not to send me on my way, but to invite me as a guest *inside* their home. One of the sons helped carry my bike up the stairs and gave up his bed so the traveler could have one.

I winced as another shot from the hose hit me in the chest. I wagged my finger at the old woman, accusing her of having better aim than she claimed. She laughed.

It was inconceivable to me that the family I had eaten lunch with that afternoon—whose children I'd juggled for—wish this woman were dead. She and her family are Muslims. They are Croats.

The house the Croatian family live in once belonged to Muslims who fled when the Croat troops shelled Mostar. The house the woman with the hose lives in once belonged to a Croatian family who fled when Muslim troops retaliated.

Wouldn't it be ironic, I thought, if the two families I'd spent time with that day were unknowingly living in each other's homes.

As a foreigner and a traveler, I am able to pass back and forth between the two (or three) camps without being threatened or asked to take sides. In each I hear stories of the other: I play soccer with a boy whose father was killed by a Serbian mine. I drink a beer with a man whose girlfriend was killed by a Muslim sniper. I talk with a family whose daughter was raped and killed by Croat troops. I'm surrounded by the effects and destruction of war, but I treat the stories as a strange sort of science fiction, because I don't want to believe they're true.

The peace is holding on, but so is the hatred.

I toweled off after hosing down, trying to get all the soap out of my ears. I drank Turkish coffee and showed the three families photos of my own. I gave and was given several hugs good night.

Then I did what I've done every night since I entered Bosnia. I slept with the enemy.

# Border Games

I was on a time schedule to get back to Budapest, and the bridge at Bosanska Gradiska in Bosnia which spans the Sava River to Croatia was my short cut. Denying my right to cross were two Serb Policemen. Presenting my case were a Polish U.N. police officer and an interpreter from Belgrad.

I listened without comprehension as they argued back and forth, already anticipating the outcome The Serbs had guns, my advocates did not. My hunch was right and the interpreter turned and apologized. I would not be allowed to cross.

One hundred and twenty kilometers back I had tried to avoid this scenario, asking a British Information Officer if I could cross the border at Bosanska Gradiska. Everyone in the office agreed it would not be a problem.

What I hadn't known then was how little the U.N. troops communicated with one another. The French were in Sarajevo, the Americans in Tusla, the Canadians in Bihac, and the Hungarians North of Banja Luka. I had seen more of Bosnia on my bicycle than most of the troops, who were confined to their sectors, had seen.

Back at the border there was talk of trying to smuggle me across in a troop vehicle. "We could approach the Hungarians or the Brits," they said, "but it might take a couple of days." *Days* I didn't have. I thanked my U.N. team for their efforts and told them I was only a touring cyclist and did not want to be the cause of an international incident.

I turned my bike around and began the backtrack. In a car (or a tank) a 240 kilometer detour is an inconvenience measured in hours. On a loaded mountain bike it is a morale destroyer measured in days.

I pedaled from early morning till dark for three days—sleeping in a field, at a British military camp and on the couch of a Muslim family. I exited Bosnia via Bihac. Then it was on to Zagreb where I caught the 1AM express train into Budapest.

Why the rush? *She* had called and given me the news. There would be no meeting in Greece as promised. My girlfriend, Kat, would not be waiting for me at the Parthenon.

Instead she had accepted my revised invitation, delivered from a phone booth on the border of Italy and Croatia, and was flying into Budapest. Having never been on an overnight bicycle trip in her life, Kat would soon be arriving with my refitted old mountain bike, loaded down with her own doubts and fears, to become my travel companion.

Wonderful, exciting and *horrifying* news.

A solo traveler for seven years, can I manage being part of a duet? Can she deal with my odd travel habits, accumulated over 30,000 miles? Can our relationship survive the back roads of Romania? Only time and distance will tell, but it is *we*, not I, that cycle on from Budapest.

# Midsummer Night's Dream

Their voices filled the still night with such sweet harmony it sent chills up and down my spine. I squeezed Kat's hand and we exchanged glances and smiles. Was this real? It had all of the elements of a dream.

We were being serenaded with a French love song by an all-men's Italian chorus on a midsummer night's eve, near a Greek Catholic church on a street corner of a village in Hungary.

It all began as we attempted to look through the large keyhole of an ornate church. The groundskeeper spied us and unlocked the sanctuary. As we gazed up at the Byzantine-styled frescos painted on the walls and ceiling he went on and on about a concert. The only thing that we understood for sure (our Hungarian limited to two-word phrases almost entirely related to food) was the event was that very evening.

Was it to be a local children's choir? The history of Hungary as interpreted by a mime troop? Traveling Scottish bagpipers? We had no idea, but we took a chance and waited for evening while drinking abysmally bitter cups of coffee in the local sweet shop.

We changed into our formal attire in the city park. "Formal attire" while on a multi-month bicycle journey often consists of a *clean*, wrinkled T-shirt, shorts and sandals *with* socks.

Our under-dressed anxiety was relieved by Father Ernst, who greeted us wearing a long black robe descending to bright white sneakers.

The group of men who filed into the now crowded church were members of *Coro Monte Pasubio*, an award-winning choral group visiting from Italy. We were treated to an hour of the finest singing I have ever heard. The audience applauded enthusiastically for encore after encore.

Having secured our bicycles in the church's schoolhouse, we wandered into a restaurant after the concert. In a back room seated at an enormously long table were the members of the chorus and their local supporters. Several people waved us in and we entered to smiles and applause. News of our bicycle journey had spread.

We sat down to glasses of red wine and seltzer. Franco, one of the choir members who spoke English, acted as our interpreter as we answered questions about our trip. At one point we let slip that we were engaged. A week prior I had asked Kat to marry me as we gazed across the Danube at the grand parliament building in Budapest. We hadn't even told our parents yet. But somehow it seemed appropriate to divulge our secret to this man with the voice of an angel.

We drank more wine and listened to more songs, wishing the evening would never end.

Two of the last to leave, we exited the restaurant only to find the entire chorus gathered in a semicircle facing us. Franco smiled and said, "It's your fault. You told me you were engaged. Now we Italians, being romantics, must sing for you."

The basses, baritones and tenors all found their notes, then broke out in laughter after a phrase, discovering they had begun in the wrong key. The second attempt was flawless. As they serenaded us with the French ballad *Les Plaisirs (The Pleasures)*, some smiled warmly at us, others simply closed their eyes.

We were touched, awed and somewhat embarrassed all at the same time. Each of the members came up to us afterwards and wished us a safe journey and much happiness. The leader presented us with one of the group's cassette tapes and his comments brought a chorus of laughter. Franco translated, "He says you must listen to this tape before or after les plaisirs…it is a collection of our church songs after all."

Then they were on their way to Debrecen and their next engagement, leaving us to bask in the glow of our own personal midsummer night's dream.

# The Weight Of Human Kindness

The bags were enormous. Their contents: peppers, cucumbers, containers of yogurt, bread, sandwiches wrapped in tin foil, potato chips, cookies, a huge bag of cherries and to top it off, two liter bottles of soda.

It was too much. We couldn't possibly fit it all in our panniers. But we had to. We hadn't been on some insane shopping spree. These were gifts from a Hungarian family who had invited us into their home. Whose fire we'd sat around the night before roasting pork fat. Whose comfortable bed we'd slept in. We hadn't the heart or the vocabulary to refuse one item.

Before we could make our escape, their neighbor added a U.S. Military "ready-to-eat" beef stew meal wrapped in heavy brown plastic and the daughter presented Kat with a stuffed animal. "Sure. Why not? Stuff it in-between the sausages another family gave us last week."

At least we would soon enter Romania where food was scarce, travel guides had warned us. "Expect only bread and dusty bottles of pickled beets on store shelves," one stated. "Stock up on dried soup mixes," added another.

Little did we know that across the border the hospitality would get heavier. That we would purchase one jar of honey and receive two more as gifts. That each time we were invited to stay with locals, we'd leave loaded down with the weight of human kindness. Our heaviest post-breakfast haul? Eight cucumbers, a large glass bottle of 160-proof homemade plum liquor and a huge slab of pork fat.

Weight is a serious issue for touring cyclists. It's not like overpacking your 4x4. Each extra pound teams up with the law of gravity to make life miserable, especially when climbing mountain passes. I've been known to read a novel, cutting out and discarding chapters as I go. But when you stuff 20 pounds of edible gifts in your packs, the fact that you've cut part of the handle off your toothbrush to conserve weight becomes laughably insignificant.

One solution is to toss what we don't need. But we're talking gifts here. You can't throw away gifts! What about redistributing them to others? Easier said than done. I attempted to offer a group of teenagers our unwanted bottles of soda. They thought I was trying to sell them and walked away.

One family gave me an old Swiss army knife. I already had one, so a few days later when it came time to say good-bye to yet another hospitable family, I presented it to the son. My weight-reduction celebration lasted less than a minute as he returned with a gift for me…a larger, heavier knife. It is still sitting at the bottom of one of my packs, for fear that if I give it away I'll get a full cutlery set in return.

Of course, we could always refuse the gifts initially and be known throughout Eastern Europe as "those ungrateful Americans." After much debate and discussion, we have agreed upon a solution that allows us to continue our journey without offending anyone. We've applied for heavy vehicle permits.

# The Thief

Weighing in at slightly under five pounds, it was the most beautiful loaf of bread we had ever seen; a dense, round loaf with a thick golden brown crust, the prize of an entire morning's labor.

Buying a loaf of bread is usually not an adventure. You'd think that it would be as simple as cycling along until we saw a bakery, but this was Northern Romania and the small villages we were pedaling through attract little tourist traffic. Why go to all of the trouble of putting up a sign when everyone in town already knows where the bakery is?

We located the word for bread in our phrase book—spelled "p-i-i-n-e" with one of those upside down "v's" over the first "i"—but we were perplexed on how to pronounce it With our first attempt an old woman's eyes lit up and she gave us directions which led us three kilometers out of town to the river. We still haven't figured out what she thought we said.

Back in town we located another woman carrying a loaf of bread. We cycled up pointing and smiling at her loaf, the woman understood that we wanted *her* bread. She clutched it close to her body and walked away.

Just as we were about to give up and drink our jar of honey, a woman on her way to church understood our plight and directed us to the "Bruteria." It was there that we found our prize, so large we had to put it in a plastic shopping bag and strap it to my bike.

While looking for somewhere to sit and enjoy our feast, we stopped at a small shop (called a "magazine" in Romania). When the owner discovered we were from America, he invited us in for coffee. We hesitated. From inside the store we wouldn't be able to see our bikes. Normally in a village as small as this one we wouldn't think of being so cautious, but this was Romania and we had been warned about Gypsy thieves a thousand times. The owner saw our concern and posted a little boy outside to guard the bikes.

While we sipped our coffee, made with the hottest tap water available, some local men stopped in for their morning whiskey. They too warned us repeatedly to watch out for Gypsies—they'd steal our bikes if we left them unattended even for a few seconds. These warnings came with a full pantomime show, acted out for us in the cramped shop.

Suddenly the boy burst in the door, his eyes wide with terror. "Our bikes!" we immediately thought. While being warned of the Gypsies, we had lost everything to them.

We ran out, hearts pounding, only to find our bikes exactly were we had parked them. Why was the boy so upset? The *bread*. It was gone. How fortunate we thought, to learn our lesson and lose so little.

Then we looked across the street and laughed. The little boy laughed too. So did the men. Then came a wave of embarrassment. We had jumped so quickly to the stereotypical conclusion. For staring at us was not a band of Gypsy thieves, but a local dairy cow, contentedly chewing our prized loaf of bread.

# Sick And Tired

On a dark, dreary day we cycled into Suceava in a cold rain. A gray factory loomed in the distance. As we approached the bridge, I heard a crash and a sharp cry behind me. Kat had fallen. Her wheels had skidded out from under her as she tried to avoid a pot hole.

She got up (leaving her bike in the street), walked to the side of the road, knelt down and burst into tears. She was covered with mud and road grit. I held her as her body shook from both sobs and laughter. "This is too much," she said. "Please tell me this will end soon."

She wasn't speaking of our adventure, but of the illness that was attacking her intestines.

As a traveler, you leave on every trip hoping and praying this won't happen. You take what precautions you can, but on a bike trip through Eastern Europe, you can't always drink purified mineral water and eat and stay in accredited hotels. We'd drunk from wells and farm house taps. We'd eaten meals with bits of meat and globs of fat we couldn't identify, and we'd slept in drafty barns and open fields.

We had hoped that Kat's illness would run its course. But after a week it was only getting worse. Severe stomach cramps followed every meal. Add, lousy weather and the constant jarring and shaking from Romania's mountainous back roads, and you have all of the makings of a travel nightmare.

Having to seek medical attention in a foreign country ranks as one of the top travel fears. Horror stories of dirty needles and unsanitary conditions abound. But travel fear or not, it was time to see a doctor.

The problem remained; where to find a good one? And one that spoke English. Then I remembered the monastery at Sucevita. There we had met a doctor who had made the journey to have his car blessed. He had been in two accidents in two months and thought it was time for some divine intervention.

We had watched as the orthodox priest chanted rapidly, then sprinkled holy water on the dash, the tires, the engine and finally, in the trunk.

As our good fortune had it, the village where the doctor and his wife worked was on our route. After directions from the gas station attendant we found ourselves in his waiting room.

The doctor was so excited and surprised to see us, that he left several patients waiting while he and his wife served us orange soda.

We thought we would be in and out in fifteen minutes, but our doctor's "visit" spanned six hours and two meals. It was more like a Sunday brunch with "duration of cramps" and "color of stool" thrown in.

We left late in the evening having easily conquered another travel fear, and laughed as we packed our bikes. Where else but Romania could you leave a doctor's office carrying prescription drugs *and* a doggy bag?

# No Forwarding Address

The burly, bearded man at the market moved quickly from behind his produce stand and intercepted me. Our loaded bikes announced "foreign travelers" and he was curious. But it wasn't until I told him where we were from that his excitement raised to a feverish pitch. His eyes grew wide as he announced to the gathering crowd, "America," grabbing me around the shoulders in a one-armed bear hug.

His Romanian I didn't understand, but I interpreted his animated gestures. His fat thumb and clenched fist went up towards his open mouth—there would be drinks. His belly shook—there would be dancing at the local disco. He made a grand gesture towards his stall, promising all of the tomatoes I could carry. Then he made a writing motion on the palm of his hand. All of these things offered in exchange for my address, for a contact in the land of the dollar, a dreamland seen weekly (with subtitles) on Romanian TV in the sunny beaches and perfect tanned bodies of *Baywatch*, and around the clock in music videos, movies, and advertisements. Every 3rd T-shirt in Romania is emblazoned with "America" or "U.S.A."—the land where everybody is rich and drives an expensive car, when not lounging pool-side while making business deals with a cellular phone.

One man literally kissed the postcard of Seattle we gave him. He and his wife had won the lottery for two of the limited number of work visas to Canada. But their dream was shattered when they could not raise the $3,000 fee per person the Romanian government required.

We had cycled through dozens of postcard-worthy villages and towns in Romania. Towns devoid of youth for lack of jobs. It was rare to see anybody between the ages of eighteen and thirty-five. Most were off to the big city of Bucharest to try their luck there. Every young person I talked to would immigrate if given the opportunity. Without travel restrictions and the visa lottery, the country would be empty overnight.

Once confined by Ceausescu and the Communist government, Romanians are now imprisoned by their country's poor economic state. It is rare for the average Romanian to be granted a visa to travel to neighboring countries in Europe, let alone the U.S. Here you quickly learn that international travel is not a right, but a granted privilege shared by few.

A contact, a postal address or phone number in America can bring the impossible dream one step closer.

To some I gladly give my address and truly hope to see them one day in Seattle. But I must be discreet because I cannot afford to house the masses. So, although the burly man persisted, I declined his offers, finally turning my back to him. And yes, it felt cold, callous, and unfair. But the reality is, as an American, I am free to venture off towards Greece, while he is left to dream from behind a mound of rotting tomatoes.

# Grandma and Grandpa Bunea

It was 10AM on a Sunday morning. The unpaved main street of the village of Noul Roman was quiet. All the cows and goats had been led out to pasture hours before.

The woman firmly grasping Kat's hand as we walked was Maria (a.k.a. Grandma). Although 70 years old and permanently hunched over from osteoporosis, she was still a fireplug of energy. Her appearance reminded me of a cute apple doll you buy at the fair. But an apple doll that could knock back a shot of plum whiskey like a sailor.

I walked behind them with Maria's husband—"Mr. Bunea" everyone called him. The former unofficial leader of the village sported a full head of shocking white hair and an expanding belly. These two people had worked their way into our hearts faster than Maria could scamper up the ladder to the hay loft to gather eggs in her apron.

We were on our way to church. Normally, we wouldn't think of attending, our wardrobe of shorts and T-shirts far from appropriate. But we were decked out in traditional Romanian costumes—brilliant, white garments with black and yellow embroidered trim. Grandma had dressed us out of a grand wooden trunk in the attic.

The church we entered was small and newly painted. The congregation is segregated, so Kat and Grandma stood on one side of the church while Mr. Bunea and I were awarded squeaky wooden seats on the men's side. News of our visit whispered its way around the sanctuary in the words, "America" and "bicicleta's."

The Orthodox liturgy hasn't changed in over a thousand years. It was easy to close my eyes and be transported back 400 years to the time when the grand churches of Bokovina were painted. A few weeks back we had visited those churches. The Frescos covering most surfaces, inside and out, are a treasure of 16th-century art. But those churches were hollow and lifeless. In Noul Roman's church we were surrounded by life. The smell of plaster and wood mixed with perspiration and cologne, while the sounds of creaking pews and clinking offertory coins mixed with the priests incantations. We left carrying the traditional offerings of bread and luminaries. We were immediately ushered back in to attend a christening—a cultural experience far more moving than any museum we'd ever visited.

The village of Noul Roman will never warrant a mention in any travel guidebook, but long after our vision of Bukovina's monasteries fade, we will remember Noul Roman's little church and hear Mr. Bunea's salutation—"William. Katy. Senetate."

A famous Romanian poet once wrote, "eternity is found in the village." I know now, exactly what he meant.

# Back To School

I always hated the first day of school when I was a kid. The transition to first grade was the worst. I was petrified of "not knowing." Not knowing if I would fit in or if my yellow submarine lunch box would be considered cool or dorky. Not knowing where I would sit or who would talk to me. I wanted to be back in the familiar surroundings of Mrs. Hathaway's kindergarten class.

But after a few days (and a new lunch box), first grade was ever-so-much cooler than kindergarten and I relaxed into my second-row seat behind my new friend, Jorgen.

That same fear visited me when we crossed the border from Romania to Bulgaria. I crossed from a country where after a month of cycling, I felt very comfortable, to a country as daunting as Mrs. Burger's first-grade classroom.

In Bulgaria, I was demoted to the "slow learners" group. I didn't know my numbers. I didn't know how to ask for bread or properly say "hello." (I thought I knew how to say "thank you," but blank stares of incomprehension were the only response I got.) Hell, I didn't even know how to read, as Bulgarian is written in Cyrillic script. It was back to phonics lessons.

Bulgaria was hot, brown and dirty. I saw fields of dying sunflowers, trash on the side of the road, homes without flower gardens. Little kids and old women peered suspiciously from behind doors. The August heat beat down and reflected off the pavement and the communist-era concrete block apartment buildings.

I wanted to be back in the green hills of Transylvania where I knew how to ask for directions and order coffee (with milk). Where I knew my numbers well enough to haggle the price if need be, and where I could at least pronounce the road signs.

Then yesterday, after my twenty-third attempt at saying "thank you" in Bulgarian, the merchant grinned, almost smiled, as he handed back my change, and a family waved when I said "good day." I had been understood.

Soon thereafter I began to notice the beautiful groves of oak trees in between the brown fields. I enjoyed the unique sound the wooden cart wheels made as they wobbled down the rutted pavement. Looks of suspicion I now viewed as curiosity and flowers appeared where none had been before.

Just as in first grade, reality hadn't changed, only the way I looked at it.

Today it is back to school. We are learning how to count. Our teachers are a group of Bulgarian school kids who laugh with us at our mistakes. Today we will learn to count to ten, and Bulgaria will be a cooler, greener, more friendly country for it.

# Muxi

"That road is impossible," the old man had warned us, tapping his index finger on our map as scores of tourists shuffled by on the pedestrian mall. We didn't laugh in his face. We waited until he was out of sight. Impossible? The road we planned to cycle in Southern Bulgaria crossed less-than-ominous roads and was clearly marked as paved on our map. He obviously had not grown up in the age of hi-tech mountain bikes.

If we had only taken the time and minimal effort to ask him why the road was impossible, he might have mentioned...the flies—"muxi" (moo-hi) in Bulgarian.

As we cycled inland from the Black Sea coast and into the oak forests, they descended upon us—not a couple, not dozens, but swarms in biblical-plague proportions. About half the size of a common house fly, they circled our heads in thick, black-pepper clouds, seeking out ears, mouths, tear ducts and nostrils. They seemed to be attracted to two things—movement and sweat. Cycling up the mountain grades, we were the perfect movable feast. But we dined as well, inhaling some and choking on a few more.

We finally resorted to covering our faces with bandannas, leaving only slits to see through. This solved all but the worst of our problems...the constant buzzing. Not the whine of gnats or the low drone of bees, it was more like a chorus of baritone mosquitoes singing an opera from Hell.

Our only relief came when we pedaled downhill as the flies' top speed was 14 kilometers per hour. But the descents were short-lived and at the bottom we needed only to count, "One, two...excuse me, these were Bulgarian flies...edno, dvei, tri," and they were back. Buzzing. Buzzing. Buzzing.

To avoid going mad, I attempted to enter a Zen-like state. To become one with the flies. To will my body not to sweat. I repeatedly sang a ditty from my childhood as a mantra:

*"Shoo fly don't bother me.*

*Muxi don't bother me.*

*Shoo fly don't bother me,*

*for I'm in love with somebody"*

But then I recalled stories of animals driven over cliffs by hoards of flies. Would this buzzing ever stop? Was it possible we'd have to endure this till Albania? Unable to contain myself any longer, I went into a frenzied swatting session, attempting to kill them all, which sent my bike swerving. Still the buzzing continued, hour after hour.

I have always preferred traveling by bicycle because it allows you to experience a country with all of your senses. In a car, the scenery often passes by like a video on fast-forward. But now I envied those who passed in cars, driving through the beautiful oak forests in air-conditioned comfort, while listening to the soundtrack of their choice.

We stopped in a small village and talked with a forester there. He said the flies were so bad, he had to wear goggles when working in the woods. Hoping for some encouraging news, we asked how long the fly season lasted. Days? Weeks? Maybe we could camp and wait them out. Our spirits sank with his reply, "They're like this all summer long."

We got back on our bikes and "edno, dvei…damn" they were back. We refitted our bandannas and pedaled on—dreaming of barking dogs, whining children, honking cars, lawn mowers, jet skis, anything…*anything*, but the song of the muxi.

# Razor Burn

Lengthy, multi-county, multilingual journeys present a traveler with daily challenges: asking directions; shopping in the market; and inquiring, "Where is the toilet?" They also present occasional challenges such as ordering in a restaurant or sending parcels back home. Before I discovered a fail-proof method, one task I used to avoid at all costs was getting a haircut.

Let's face it, if you screw-up ordering a meal you may pay with heartburn that lasts, at most, a day. But a bad haircut lingers for weeks, months even. The problem lies in the endless interpretations of phrases like, "just a trim" and "keep the sideburns."

Throughout my travels, I've discovered that nearly every barber on the planet owns an electric razor. Each comes with a set of guides, numbered 1 to 4, based on how much (or little) hair they leave behind. No. 1 is the shortest (marine recruit length) and No.4 is the longest (still extremely short, but fuzzy objects no longer cling to your head as if it were Velcro).

With this knowledge I can simply hold up four fingers and point to the razor, showing that I want the back and sides buzzed. Then with a gesture I can show I'd like a little trimmed off the top. This allows me to get the same practical, semi-fashionable haircut in Budapest as I would in Bombay without uttering a single word.

Recently, in Blagoevgrad, Bulgaria, 20 kilometers east of the Macedonian border, I decided it was time for my traveler's cut. I overheard someone speaking English at a café and asked her where I might find a good barber. She told me I was in luck, because the best hair stylist in the city worked across the street.

I entered the shop, wary of the prices, and asked how much it would cost to get my hair cut—not shampooed or styled or blown dry—simply cut. I was shocked. When converted to U.S. currency, the price came to less than 75 cents. Not only was I about to receive one of the finest haircuts of my life, but one of the cheapest as well.

My stylist, a slender woman in her twenties, immediately understood my speechless instructions and grabbed for her clippers and popped in the No. 4 attachment. With confidence, I leaned back in the chair and paged through the Bulgarian equivalent of *People* magazine. She quickly finished with the razor and went to work trimming with scissors.

Halfway through, I noticed she kept combing my hair forward. I caught her attention and with a gesture showed that I normally combed my hair back, then I returned to an in-depth article about one of Cher's ex-husbands.

The razor was back on and had cut a wide swath the middle of my head before I could protest. She had interpreted my gesture differently. She thought I had changed my mind and now wanted my whole head shaved. There was nothing I could do but watch the hair fall, trying not to look shocked as large chunks fell into my lap. It wasn't her fault, after all.

My fail-proof method had failed and I looked in the mirror at a style three-sixteenths of an inch shy of Jay Buhner's.

I forced a smile as I paid my bill, gave her a tip…and reached for my baseball cap.

# Highway Robbery

The knife came into full view and three men blocked our way on a lonely stretch of highway seven kilometers outside of Kukes, Albania. My initial thought was not one of fear, but "I wonder if we'll loose our bikes?"

Without warning, clubs emerged and they attacked—90 seconds of confused, absolute horror, followed by stunned silence and tears. We stood bruised and bloodied in the middle of the road, watching the robbers flee up into the scraggy mountain brush with our cameras, passports and 19 dollars in cash.

We were alive. The worst was over. Or so we thought.

The policeman arrived at the scene of the crime 45 minutes later…on a bus. We had long since been helped by passersby.

After assessing the situation, he realized he had a problem. He needed to get Kat and me and our bikes back to the police station, but he had no vehicle. Easily solved. He simply pointed his gun and stopped the first truck that came our way and accused the driver of being involved in the crime. This was Northern Albania, the Wild West of Europe, where nothing made sense or had a sense of order. The driver had no choice but to become an unwilling civil servant and drive us back into town.

At the police station, cigarette smoke filled the drab concrete interrogation room as more and more men squeezed their way in. The noise level grew as they bickered amongst themselves, trying to get a better look at the Americans. Kat's head had begun to bleed again, but no one would respond to my pleas to get a cloth or bandage. I finally took off my T-shirt and handed it to her. More smoke and more noise. I couldn't take it any more. I stood up and whistled, yelling at them to shut-up and go away. It didn't matter what I said. They couldn't understand a word, but now they spoke in muffled tones and several shuffled out of the room.

The chief entered, dragging another reluctant civil servant—our interpreter—a local business man who had the misfortune of being fluent in English. The chief sat across from us and set down a single sheet of white paper. Now we could get down to serious police work.

He asked us to tell him exactly what happened. For the next 45 minutes, through our interpreter, we recalled our story. During this time he wrote exactly three words on the sheet of paper. What were they? Bread, milk, eggs? Who knows.

All the while a typist sat at the other end of the table with his arms folded. The chief asked one final question. "Is anyone in this room involved in the crime?" The poor truck driver cowered in the corner. We quickly cleared his name.

The chief stood up, satisfied with his three-word report and exited the room, followed by most of the others. Thank God it was over. The typist now inserted a form in triplicate and asked us to tell him exactly what had happened. It started all over again.

In the midst of our second marathon questioning session I leaned over to Kat and asked, "90 more seconds with the robbers, or four and a half more hours with the police, which would you choose?"

The wonderful and horrible thing about adventures is, you are not allowed to pick and choose which elements you'll experience. The insanity of the police station and the emotions and images wrapped up in those ninety seconds on the highway were so intense and loom so large, they threaten to drown out all other memories of our trip like a loud siren piercing an otherwise peaceful night.

What now?

Did we want to continue our journey in Albania and risk another robbery, or worse?

It would be so easy to get on the first bus or train heading for Athens. We could be on a flight back home and leave it all behind.

We had a decision to make.

# Heading for Home

We walked in through the high-walled gate, through double sets of thick, lead doors and up to the counter at the U.S. Embassy in Tirana, Albania. Having been beaten and robbed, we needed new passports. We asked the woman behind the counter where we could get photos taken and where we could use a fax. She had no idea. "What have other Americans done who have been in the same situation?" we asked. "You don't understand. Americans don't travel in Albania, especially in the region you were in. It's too dangerous."

We'd heard this before. The sons of the family who took care of us after the robbery made us promise we would do no more cycling in Albania. While our bodies still ached, it was easy to comply with their wish. We were scared. But after a couple of days when we arrived to pick up our passports, we were reconsidering.

To not get back on the bikes was to admit defeat—to allow the thieves to steal much more than passports, cameras and money. Would we allow them to steal our adventurous spirits as well?

We took the train to the coast to avoid the insane drivers of Tirana and got back on our bikes. We pedaled along the coast, gazing out at the blue-green water which led to islands and, somewhere out there, Italy.

That night as we set up our tent on a flat patch of rocky ground far from the highway, you could feel the tension. Finally, Kat broke the silence. "Tell me we're going to be OK." For the first time in my travel career, I looked out at desolate mountains and I was afraid. I hated the thieves for that feeling so much more than for the bumps and bruises.

The morning brought clear skies and a little less fear. Our coastal road was not without tensions, however. Little kids threw rocks at us when they weren't throwing rocks at goats...or each other. People laughed as their dogs chased us and one motorist drove straight at us, only to swerve to avoid us at the last second. He smiled back at us...only joking.

Albania had a rawness to it I've felt no where else. It was the best and the worst of our trip concentrated down to a few days. Never had I seen such beauty as in its rugged mountains and coastline. The hospitality of people who took us in rivaled that of any country in Eastern Europe. But with that rawness came a tension, a sense of danger that rarely left us.

By the time we cycled into Saranda and took the ferry to the island of Corfu in Greece, we were ready for some well deserved R & R.

A couple of weeks and a few beaches and islands later, we walked through the gates of the Acropolis in Athens. "What is the date?" Kat asked as we gazed up at the columns of the Parthenon. It was September 30— only three days later than we had planned to meet, back when I was on a solo journey.

We had been through so much together: sickness, storms, fatigue and fear. Thousands of kilometers of winding dusty roads that led to villages, vistas and people we will never forget.

But now it was time to find a travel agent and a cheap airline ticket, buy a few souvenirs, box the bikes and head for home.

Our trip was over, but our adventure continues…for sometime soon in Seattle, surrounded by family and friends, my travel companion will become my wife.

# Acknowlegements

Solo adventures are rarely solo.

I would like to thank Brian Higham and the entire staff at public radio station, KUOW, who first aired my aerograms sent from India; Jim Molnar of *The Seattle Times* who acknowledged the writer in me; and Allen Noren, who originally edited the South Africa pieces, for a constant flow of advice and encouragement.

For help with this manuscript, my heart-felt appreciation goes to Jeff Weir, Michele De William, and Susan Motte for their invaluable hours of editing and proofing. And thanks to Jerry Mills at Digital Image for his prepress expertise.

For equipment and support special thanks go to: Estelle Grey and Dan Towle at R+E Cycles for parts and supplies and my always dependable Rodriguez mountain bike; Jeff Scully at NewSport for the Ortleib water-proof panniers; Steve Smilanick at S and S Machine for the amazing bicycle frame couplers, and Joe Wadden at Outdoor Research for first-aid and camping supplies.

A lifetime of thanks to Mom and Dad, who have encouraged me in every endeavor, no matter how crazy; to my brother, Jeff, whom I still write for and my sister-in-law, Julie, for putting up with the phone bills; to Leo DiLorenzo, my unofficial twin, for keeping my adventurous spirit alive; to Michael Pace, whose house and hospitality have always been open; to Randy and Laura Franz and Jorie Wackerman for friendship and free storage space; to Janis Levine for brainstorming and a cold beer in Tikal.

For help in many ways; Susan Ronn and Biff Fouke, David Branch, David and Stacya Silverman, Laurie Clothier, Tom and Katie Bloom, Bill Weir, Monica Plagemann, Steve Young and Noni Roblin, Dave and Sharva Maynard, Thomas and Jill Schroeder, Gorden Black, Rick Steves, Jeff and Cindy Hoyt, Mark Cole, Andrew and Annie Traister, Herb and Karen Kavet, Barb and Scott Loners, and so many others too numerous to mention.

And to Kat Marriner—book designer, layout artist, publisher, friend, travel companion and wife—life and this book would not be complete without you.

# About the Author

Willie Weir is known to public radio listeners for his commentaries aired on KUOW in Seattle, Washington. His bicycle travels have taken him throughout the U.S., Canada, Mexico, Central America, New Zealand, India, South Africa, and the Balkans. Willie gives presentations about bicycle touring and his journeys to thousands of kids and adults each year, hoping to spur on new adventurers and bicycle advocates.

An actor by training, Willie has performed on stage in everything from Shakespeare to musical comedy.

He lives in Seattle with his wife, Kat, listening for the road to beckon, as it always does.

Photo by Kat Marriner

# *Share the Adventure...*

Please send additional copies of **Spokesongs** to:

Name: _____

Address: _____

Address: _____

City/State/ZIP _____

_____ books at $11.95         _____

WA state residents add 8.2% sales tax         _____

Shipping ($2.00 for the first book,
$1.00 for each additional book)         _____

Total         _____

Make your checks payable to: *Pineleaf Productions*
Mail to: *7812 Stone Avenue N*
*Seattle, WA 98103*

*PineleafPr@aol.com*

Contact publisher for group discounts